THE PROFESSIO TO

HAIF
HAIRSTYLES

THE PROFESSIONAL'S ILLUSTRATED GUIDE TO

HAIRCARE & HAIRSTYLES

WITH 280 STYLE IDEAS AND STEP-BY-STEP TECHNIQUES

NICKY POPE

Photography by David Goldman

HERMES HOUSE

To all my friends in the professional hairdressing industry who have looked after me so well.

This edition is published by Hermes House, an imprint of Anness Publishing Ltd, Blaby Road, Wigston, Leicestershire LE18 4SE
Email: info@anness.com
Web: www.hermeshouse.com; www.annesspublishing.com

Publisher: Joanna Lorenz
Senior Editor: Lucy Doncaster
Designer: Simon Daley
Photography: David Goldman
Illustrator: Vanessa Card
Production Controller: Christine Ni

Bracketed terms are intended for American readers.

AUTHOR'S NOTE
Special thanks for their encouragement and help to Louise Wood and Susan Pope for being my second eyes, and to Tim Frisby for getting me started. I'm grateful to Lucy Doncaster for being unflappable, patient and very good at what she does.

CONTENTS

How to use this book

How you wear your hair and the way it makes you look and feel is incredibly important. Whether hair is groomed, worn loose and casual, or even remains unkempt, do remember that its look, colour, texture and style is all part of your individuality.

Although genetic factors determine the type, natural colour and texture of your hair, the rest is down to you. The way you live your life, your state of health and your haircare regime will impact on the overall appearance of your hair and its capacity to shine, move and look vital.

For many centuries women all over the world have been changing the colour of their hair, originally using dyes made from natural sources such as henna and, in modern times, from chemical colourants, although natural dyes are still popular.

The desire to curl or wave straight hair or smooth out natural curls is also pervasive in most cultures, and as new techniques and tools develop, the power of a hairstyle to entirely change a person's look becomes ever more apparent – it's almost a magical way to reinvent an identity.

It's no surprise, then, that so many women spend time and energy in getting their hair to look a certain way, and stay like that. From hours in the bathroom, washing, fixing and styling hair, to countless trips to the salon for cut, colour and waving services, it seems that hair and hairdressing is bigger business than ever. But with so much advice available, so many products and such a choice of hairstyling tools and equipment spilling off shelves in the shops, it's not quite so easy to figure out what to do for the best! How will you know what style is right for you? How should you care for your hair and makes sure every day is a good hair day?

The answers lie in understanding your hair and learning to manage it well, and this beautiful book tells everything you will ever need to know about your hair, from basic care to styling and dressing it yourself so that you can be confident that your hair looks fantastic each time you step out of the door.

The book opens with basic information about healthy hair, including guidance to help you assess your own hair, its texture and type, and understand how to tackle problems in the short- and long-term so that you will be better able to keep it in great condition. By looking at the structure of different hair types, and considering the impact of diet, lifestyle and different care regimes, you will learn what to do for your particular type. Problems that occur naturally or arise through medical illness can be tackled and we explain how to recognize various conditions and what action to take.

Good haircare regimes are essential to looking fabulous and we teach you how to establish good routines, cope with wayward or damaged hair, and how to use both manufactured and natural products to look after your hair properly. This is especially important as your hair

Left: *Regard your hair as an asset. Shiny, healthy hair dressed to suit your individual look is an important part of your personal style.*

ages and its condition and appearance changes, or when external factors such as the sun, wind, heat and pollution have an impact on your hair. We have a happy holiday guide to enable you to provide the correct care for your hair in all weathers.

There then follows a chapter on successful styling, including advice and ideas on how to select a salon that's right for you, and what to expect when you get there – from levels of service to understanding what your hairdresser is talking about.

Processes such as colouring, perming and straightening are also demystified, with advice on how to get the best results both at home and from salon services.

A series of illustrated style galleries to help you choose the perfect look come next. Successful styling comes from picking a cut to suit your look, and it is important that you can maintain it with ease. From short to mid-length or long, and straight to curly, our pages of more than 160 styles will give you plenty of ideas.

You will need to know how to keep working that style to best effect and the chapter on styling tools and techniques comprehensively explains what to use and when, together with valuable information on styling and finishing products. Forget indecision and feelings of panic as you gain an insight into superb styling for every occasion.

There are also pages of clearly illustrated step-by-step explanations for a range of styling techniques, from basic blow-dries to straightening, curling and setting hair in a variety of ways, using rods, bendies, curlers and pins. You can practise affixing temporary hair, too, including ponytails, flashes of colour and full wigs.

Above *Learn how to wear accessories, hats and ornaments in a way that balances your face shape and works with your dress style.*

Having laid the foundations, the book continues by exploring ways of dressing hair, with clear step-by-step photographs and more than 85 projects you can do at home. These range from easy ideas for casual daywear through to slick work styles and then on to party nights and special occasions, from red carpet dos to wedding days.

Having revealed the secrets of how to achieve perfect hairstyles, it makes sense to consider how best to wear a hat to suit your hair, and we show you how to select something just right, as well as how to make your own headpiece. Accessories such as flowers, bows and clips, scarves and headbands are another great way to enhance a hairstyle and we share ideas on what to wear and how to fix it to your hair for a stylish finish.

Hair is a good indicator of your health and state of mind, so enjoy its potential and bring out the best in yourself. Learn to love your hair and wear it with style.

Left *Practise good haircare and follow a styling routine to keep your hair looking in great condition at all times.*

Healthy hair

Beautiful, shining hair can and should make you look and feel great. It is a versatile fashion accessory, and you can change its colour, texture, shape and length to suit your mood and personal style. In order to maintain optimum health of your hair, however, you need to know what impact environmental stresses will have on its condition and shine, including the damage caused by over-exposure to sun, wind, air-conditioning or central heating. It's equally important to maintain a balanced diet and good haircare and styling routines to ensure your hair is your natural crowning glory.

What is hair?

Understanding the structure of hair and how it forms will give you a better grasp of how to achieve healthy hair. Armed with this knowledge, you can go on to improve the condition of your own hair and pinpoint any particular problems you may have.

A human hair consists mainly of a protein called keratin, which is also found in your nails. It also contains some moisture as well as trace metals and minerals that are found in the rest of the body. The visible part of the hair, called the shaft, is dead tissue: the only living part of the hair is its root, called the dermal papilla, which lies snugly below the surface of the scalp in a tube-like depression known as the hair follicle. The dermal papilla is made up of cells that are fed by the bloodstream in the skin.

Each hair consists of three layers. The outer layer, or cuticle, is the hair's protective shield and has tiny overlapping scales, rather like tiles on a roof. When the cuticle scales lie flat and neatly overlap the hair feels silky-soft and looks glossy. If the cuticle scales have been physically or chemically damaged or broken, however, the hair will be dull and brittle and will tangle easily.

Under the cuticle lies the cortex, which is made up of fibre-like cells that give hair its strength and elasticity. The cortex also contains the pigment called melanin, which gives hair its natural colour.

At the centre of the hair is the medulla, consisting of soft keratin cells interspersed with spaces. The function of the medulla is not known, but it may carry nutrients and other substances to the cortex and cuticle. This could explain why hair is affected so rapidly by changes in general health.

Why does hair shine?

Hair's natural shine is a result of sebum, which is an oil composed of waxes and fats that contains a natural antiseptic that helps fight infection. Sebum is produced by the sebaceous glands present in the dermis (the skin). These glands are linked to the hair follicles and release sebum into them. As a lubricant, sebum gives an excellent protective coating to the entire hair shaft, smoothing the cuticle scales and helping hair retain its natural moisture and elasticity.

The smoother the surface of the cuticle, the more light will be reflected from the hair and, therefore, the higher the level of hair shine will be. This is why it is more difficult to obtain a shine on curly hair than on straight hair, as on curly hair the cuticle isn't so smooth. Under certain circumstances, such as excessive hormonal activity, the sebaceous glands produce too much sebum, and the result is oily hair. Conversely, if too little sebum is produced, the hair will be dry.

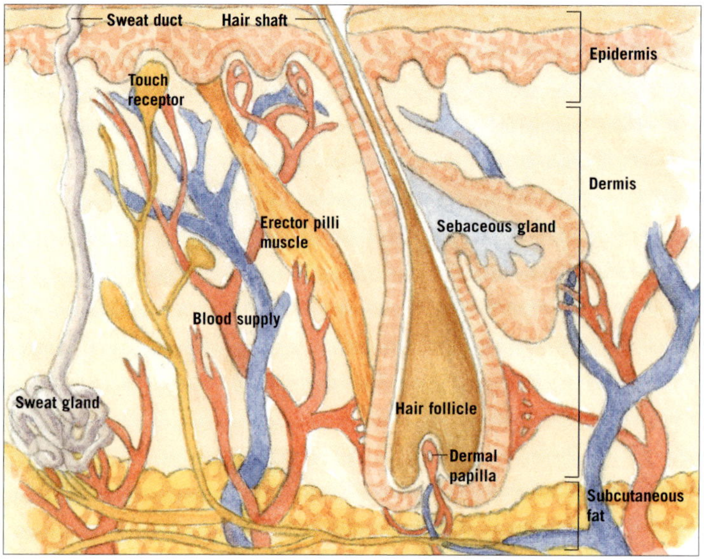

The growth cycle of hair

Hair goes through three stages of growth: the anagen phase when it actively grows, which lasts between two to four years; the catagen, or transitional phase, when the hair stops growing but cellular activity continues in the papilla, and which lasts 90–120 days; and the telogen, or resting phase, when growth stops completely. During the telogen phase there is no further growth or activity at the papilla; eventually the old hair is pushed out by the new growth and the cycle begins all over again.

At any given time, about 93 per cent of an individual's hair is in the anagen phase, 1 per cent is in the catagen phase, and 6 per cent is in the telogen phase. Scalp hair, which reacts to hormonal stimuli just like hair on the rest of the

Left *The structure of the skin is complex, comprising many elements, including hair follicles, dermal papillae and sebaceous glands.*

Did you know?

- *Hair grows about 1cm/½in per month.*
- *A single strand lives for up to seven years.*
- *If a person never had their hair cut it could grow to a length of about 107cm/42in before falling out.*
- *Women have more hair than men.*
- *Hair grows faster in the summer and during sleep.*
- *Hairs grow fastest between the ages of 16 and 24 years.*
- *Between the ages of 40 and 50 women tend to lose about 20 per cent of their hair.*
- *Hair becomes drier with age.*

body, is genetically programmed to repeat its growth cycle 24–25 times during the average person's lifetime.

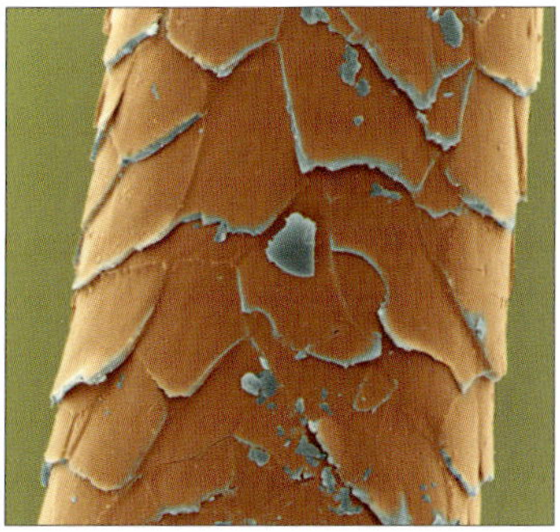

Above *The hair's cuticle is formed by overlapping scales that need to lie close and flat to allow hair to shine. Here, they are roughened, indicating brittle and dull hair.*

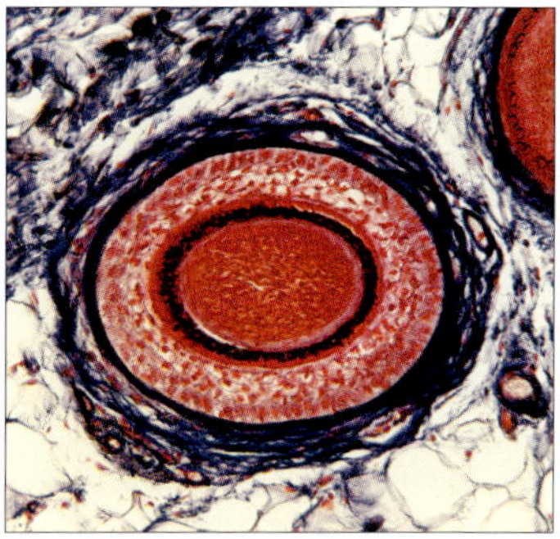

Above *The central section of the hair is called the medulla, consisting of softer keratin. Surrounding this is the cortex, which gives hair its strength and elasticity, and the cuticle.*

The importance of diet

Like the rest of the body, the health and condition of hair is dependent upon a consistently good diet, which ensures it is supplied with all the necessary nutrients for sustained growth and health.

Regular exercise is also important as it promotes good blood circulation, which in turn ensures that vital oxygen and nutrients are transported to the hair root via the blood.

Poor eating habits and lack of regular exercise are soon reflected in the state of our hair, and even a minor case of short-term ill-health can often make the hair look limp and lacklustre. Although there are many products and supplements on the market that claim to improve the condition of hair, if you eat a balanced diet containing plenty of fresh, raw ingredients, including fruit and vegetables, you shouldn't need to take any supplementary vitamins to promote healthy hair growth and condition.

Drinking plenty of water (between six and eight glasses a day), herbal teas and unsweetened fruit juice will keep you hydrated and your hair looking good.

Below *Regular exercise and good grooming routines will help keep your hair healthy.*

Tips for healthy hair

- *Cut down on tea and coffee if you can – these are powerful stimulants that act on the nervous, respiratory and cardiovascular systems, increasing the excretion of water and important nutrients. They also hamper the absorption of minerals that are crucial for hair health.*
- *Alcohol dilates blood vessels and so helps increase blood flow to the tissues, including the scalp. However, alcohol is antagonistic to several minerals and vitamins that are vital for healthy hair, so it should only be consumed in moderation.*
- *Regular exercise stimulates the circulatory system, encouraging a healthy blood supply to all cells and nourishing and helping to regenerate and repair.*
- *Any type of medication can potentially affect the condition of your hair. If you notice any dramatic change in its condition, such as significant hair loss or thinning, then you should tell your doctor as soon as possible.*

The ages of hair

As our bodies grow older, so too does our hair, and this affects the way it is produced and in what quantities, as well as its texture and type. It is important, therefore, that care regimes are adjusted accordingly depending on your age and stage.

The baby and child

A baby's hair characteristics are determined from the very moment of conception. By the 16th week of pregnancy the foetus will be covered with lanugo, a downy body hair that is usually shed before or around birth. The first hair appears on the baby's head by around the 20th week of pregnancy and it is at this time that the pigment, melanin, which will determine the colour of the hair, is first produced.

A few weeks after birth, the baby's original hair begins to fall out or is rubbed off. The new hair is quite different from the initial downy mass, so a baby born with blonde, wispy curls might have dark straight hair by the age of six months.

Cradle cap, which appears as thick, yellow scales in patches over the scalp, can be a common problem at this age. This is the result of a natural build-up of skin cells and can be gently loosened by rubbing a little baby oil on to the scalp at night and washing it off in the morning. This may need to be repeated for several days until all the scales have been removed.

Children's hair is normally in beautiful condition and is best cut and styled simply. At the onset of puberty, however, this may all change, and many young people experience oily hair and skin for the first time as a result of hormone changes.

Ageing

As we grow older our hair changes, and by the age of 30 to 40 years old some hair will grow without melanin, so be colourless. The production of melanin is governed by genetic factors, and the best indication of when your hair will become grey is the age at which your parents' hair lost its colour.

Apart from giving hair its colour, melanin also helps to soften and make each strand more flexible. This is why white hair tends to become wirier and coarser in texture. The ageing hair also loses elasticity and becomes rougher as the scalp produces less sebum.

Because the texture changes, the hair is inclined to pick up dust and smoke from the atmosphere, so it soon appears discoloured and dirty-looking. Mineral deposits from chlorinated water can give white hair a greenish tinge. Chelating, clarifying, or purifying shampoos will help to strip this build-up from the hair.

To counteract the dryness associated with ageing hair, use specially formulated richer shampoos and conditioning products on a regular basis. In addition, weekly intensive treatments are essential to counteract moisture loss.

Above *The amount of hair and hair type of a newborn child does not necessarily indicate how their hair will be as they age.*

Right *White and grey hair needs special care and products to combat dryness and restore vitality and elasticity.*

Pregnancy and post-natal hair

During pregnancy, many women feel their hair often looks its best. This is perhaps because the hormonal changes stop hair falling out at the same rate so it feels thicker. Pregnant women also have more blood coursing through their veins than usual and as it circulates it feeds the scalp to help hair become healthier. However, after the birth or after breast-feeding ceases, this thick, glossy extra hair can be lost at what may seem to many an alarming rate. What appears to be excessive hair loss is therefore simply a postponement of a natural occurrence, a condition that is known as post-partum alopecia.

Another more significant problem that may occur during pregnancy and while breast-feeding is caused by a depletion in the protein content of the hair, causing it to become drier and more brittle. Combat this by frequently using an intensive conditioning treatment.

In some women, pregnancy can affect the hair type, changing curly hair to straight or vice versa. It may then revert back to its prior condition once the baby is born, although occasionally it does not.

There's a view that it's best to avoid perming during pregnancy because the hair is in an altered state and the result can be unpredictable. However, a new colour can give your hair a lift.

The menopause and beyond

Many women report experiencing some hair loss or thinning of their hair during the menopause. This may be caused by hormone imbalances (similar to the ones during pregnancy) and will usually be temporary. Equally, emotional or physical stress, illness, medication (including synthetic hormone replacement therapy [HRT]) and thyroid problems can be to blame, or hair loss at this time in life can be hereditary.

Above *Enjoy your hair whatever your age. Understand changes in your body and adapt your haircare routine accordingly, and seek advice from a doctor if you are unhappy.*

The thinning process often ceases after the menopause, when hormone levels have stabilized, and some women experience renewed hair growth and thickness.

Easy ways to disguise thin hair include:

- Have a short, layered style to add the illusion of fullness and body.
- Blow-dry hair in the opposite direction to growth then, when it is dry, brush it back in the other direction. This helps create root lift which makes hair appear fuller.
- Avoid using combs, as they will 'snag' hair and pull it out; use soft hairbrushes instead, which are kinder on the hair.
- Use a good volumizing mousse to add body to clean hair.
- Alternate the type of shampoo you use every month.

Hair colour and texture

From striking brunettes, to the lightest of blondes, fiery redheads and stunning black, colour is an important way of enhancing your look. But what makes one head of hair so different from another? Here's a quick guide to why hair varies so much.

What determines hair colour?

Hair colour is closely related to skin colour, and both are governed by the same type of pigment, melanin. The number of these melanin granules in the cortex of the hair and the shape of these granules determine a person's natural hair colour.

In the majority of cases the melanin granules are elongated in shape. People who have a large number of elongated melanin granules in the cortex of each hair have black hair, those with slightly fewer elongated granules have brown hair, and people with even less will be blonde. In other people the melanin granules are spherical or oval rather than elongated, and this makes the hair appear red.

Combinations of spherical or oval granules, perhaps with a moderate amount of the elongated ones, will give the appearance of rich, reddish-brown tinges. If, however, spherical granules occur in combination with a large number of elongated granules, then the blackness of the hair will almost mask the redness, although it will still give a subtle tinge to the hair and differentiate it from pure black.

Below *The natural colour of hair affects its texture: blonde (bottom left) is finest, brunette (below) is slightly thicker, and red hair (bottom) is thickest.*

Above *Asian hair tends to be black and straighter, thicker and coarser than other types.*

Above *Afro hair is often naturally tightly curled and dark brown in colour.*

Above *Caucasian hair ranges from straight to curly, and from dark brown to white blonde.*

Hair colour darkens with age, but at some stage of life the pigment formation slows down. As the amount of melanin granules reduces, silvery-grey hairs begin to appear. Gradually, the production of melanin ceases and all the hair becomes colourless – which is often termed grey or white. When melanin granules are lacking from birth, as in albinos, the hair is white.

Hair texture

The natural colour of hair also affects its texture, which is determined by the diameter of each hair. Natural blondes have finer hair than brunettes, while redheads have the thickest hair. Generally speaking, hair can be divided into three categories: fine, medium, and thick and coarse, and these have certain traits:

- **Fine hair** can be strong or weak; but, because of its texture, all fine hair has the same characteristic – it lacks volume.
- **Medium hair** is neither too thick nor too thin, and is strong and elastic.
- **Thick and coarse hair** is abundant and heavy, with a tendency to grow outwards from the scalp as well as downwards. It often lacks elasticity and is frizzy.

A single head of hair may consist of several different textures. For example, fine hair is often found on the temples, and the hairline at the front and on the nape of the head, while the texture elsewhere may be medium or even coarse.

Race can determine hair texture and colour. Caucasian hair usually varies from straight to curly, while the colour ranges from dark brown to white blonde. Afro hair is usually tightly curled and dark brown, while Asian hair tends to be straight, thick, coarse and black. Mixed races will be a combination.

Did you know?

- *Healthy hair is highly elastic and can stretch 20 or 30 per cent before snapping.*
- *Chinese circus acrobats have been known to perform tricks while suspended by their hair.*
- *A human hair is stronger than copper wire of the same thickness.*
- *The combined strength of a full head of human hair is capable of supporting a weight equivalent to that of 99 people.*
- *We lose about 100 hairs a day, but as the average head has between 100,000 and 140,000 it's not a problem.*

Straight or curly?

Whether hair is curly, wavy or straight depends on two things: its shape as it grows out of the follicle; and the distribution of keratin-producing cells at the roots.

All hair grows with a twist (even when it appears to be straight) and the number of twists it takes will determine how curly it will be. For example, Afro hair has nearly 12 times as many twists as Caucasian hair.

Where the hair bulb or papilla lies in the follicle affects whether the hair grows either straighter or curlier. Where there is an even distribution of keratin cells around the bulb in the follicle, straight hair is formed. In curly hair, however, the production of keratin cells is uneven, so that at any given time there are more keratin cells on one side of the oval-shaped follicle than on the other, causing the hair to grow at an angle. In addition, the production of excess cells alternates between the sides, so the developing hair grows first in one direction and then in the other; the result is curly hair.

Define your hair type

Your hair type is determined by its natural condition – how much moisture the hair holds and its sebum levels – and how you treat your hair. Perming, colouring and heat styling can have an impact, so it is important to use the correct products.

Having established what the natural texture of your hair is, it is important to work out its type – the dryness, softness or oiliness – so that you ensure you use products that are appropriate for that type of hair.

Normal hair

This type is defined as neither oily nor dry, and has been left in its natural state. It is able to hold its style, and looks good most of the time.

Haircare Because it has not been chemically altered or damaged, normal hair may only need a conditioning treatment on an occasional basis. Choose a gentle shampoo for regular use, or you could try a two-in-one conditioning shampoo. When this dual-action product is lathered into wet hair the shampoo removes dirt, oil and styling products while the conditioner remains in the lather. As the hair is rinsed with clean water, the oil and dirt are washed away with the shampoo and conditioning droplets are released on to the hair, leaving it shiny and easier to manage.

Dry hair

This type of hair looks dull, feels dry, tangles easily, and is difficult to comb or brush, particularly when it is wet. It simply doesn't contain enough moisture, which can be because there isn't enough sebum being produced or perhaps because the hair is older and the cuticles have opened up. When this happens, the cortex is more likely to lose its moisture through exposure to excessive shampooing, overuse of heat-styling equipment, misuse of colour or perms, damage from the sun, or harsh weather conditions. Roughed-up cuticles mean the hair loses its ability to shine and the cortex may even split or break, making hair brittle.

Haircare Really damaged, dry hair cannot repair itself but you can help prevent further deterioration. For example, if your hair has become dry and lost its elasticity, bounce and suppleness it's important to use a nourishing shampoo and an intensive conditioner. Allowing hair to dry naturally whenever possible and reducing the amount of heat-styling from hairdryers and electrical styling tools will also help. Protect from further exposure to drying environments or UV rays.

Below *Hair at the roots is new and needs less conditioner, so apply to mid-lengths and ends.*

Below *Restore bounce and vitality by using a purifying cleanser to remove product overload.*

Below *Very curly hair may be dry and prone to breakage without moisturizing products.*

Oily hair

Often associated with teenagers, oily hair looks lank and greasy and needs frequent washing. It is caused by the overproduction of sebum, which can be a genetic tendency, or as a result of hormone disturbances, stress, a humid atmosphere, excessive brushing, constantly running hands through the hair, or perspiration. After cleansing, the hair becomes oily, sticky and unmanageable in a short time.

Haircare Use a gentle, non-aggressive shampoo that also gives the hair added volume. Consider a light perm, which will lift the hair at the roots and limit the dispersal of sebum. It could be worth rethinking your diet: reduce dairy fats and greasy foods. Try to eat plenty of fresh food, and drink six to eight glasses of water every day.

Did you know?

You can determine the texture of your hair by running the thumb and finger along the length of the hair from the root to the tip. Fine hair is small in diameter and feels smooth and silky along its length. Coarse hair, because of the way it is formed (a wide diameter with more raised, lifted cuticles) feels rougher to the touch. It's important to identify your hair texture in order to choose the right care and styling products.

Combination hair

This common type of hair is typified by being oily at the roots but dry and sometimes split at the ends. Not only can it look lank and flat, but it will be dull and flyaway too. The causes include a reliance on chemical treatments, the overuse of detergent-based shampoos, overexposure to sunlight, and overuse of heat-styling equipment. Such repeated abuse often provokes sebum secretion at the roots and a partial alteration in the cuticle scales, which no longer protect the cortex so the hair ends become dry.

Haircare Experiment with some of the many products on offer until you find the best ones for you. Aim for those that have only a gentle action on the hair. Excessive use of formulations intended specifically for oily hair or for dry hair may contribute to the problem. Ideally, use a product specially designed for combination hair. If this is not possible, try using a shampoo for oily hair and finish by applying a conditioner only from the middle lengths to the ends of the hair, where moisture is needed.

Above left *Hair that is well cared for will be smooth and easily combed to be tangle-free.*

Above right *Most hair is a combination of hair types so it is important to use the right products only where they are needed.*

Grey hair

This effect is primarily, but not always, linked with the ageing of the hair. The loss of colour is due to the gradual reduction in the amount of melanin granules produced. Grey hair is usually a mix of hair with and without colour (white hair is total loss of colour), and it tends to be coarser than younger hair.

Haircare Grey hair may absorb pollution and can even look yellow, so it's important to use products designed specifically for greying hair to give it additional protection from the environment.

Common problems

Many problems with the hair and scalp, whether naturally occurring or of our own making, can be addressed relatively easily. It's simply a question of understanding the causes and, where appropriate, taking specialist advice.

Above *Be kind to your hair! Stressed hair needs special attention to recover its condition.*

Damaged hair

Many people suffer from damaged hair, which is typified by being dull, lifeless, lacking in shine and difficult to manage. In many cases, unavoidable environmental factors, such as wind, sun, sand, sea water, chlorine, air-conditioning or central heating are the culprits, but excessive use of hairdryers and straightening or curling irons will also take their toll.

Even if you don't expose your hair to exterior stresses, the misuse of styling tools, including combs or hairbrushes, pins, hairgrips (bobby pins) and elastic hairbands (headbands) can damage the hair cuticle and make hair more brittle and appear less shiny. It is important, therefore, to be gentle with your hair at all times, even when you simply put it up in a ponytail, avoiding any ripping or tugging.

Chemical processes all work by changing the structure of hair in order to allow colour to penetrate or a perm solution to work. When perming or relaxing, the structure of the hair must be broken and then neutralized or restructured afterwards. This process means that chemically-altered hair is very often more porous than untreated hair, so it needs gentle cleansers and good conditioners.

Haircare Preventing damage is about keeping hair as flexible as possible with a high moisture content. Conditioning products are very effective; choose specific ones to address varying degrees of damage.

Limp hair

Fine hair tends to be limp, looks flat, and is difficult to handle because it does not hold a style. The texture of fine hair is hereditary, but the problem is often made worse by using too heavy a conditioner, which weighs the hair down. Excessive use of styling products can have the same effect.

Haircare To tackle the problem, wash hair frequently with a mild cleanser and use a very light conditioner. Volumizing shampoos can help give body, and soft perms will make hair appear thicker. Colouring hair can swell the hair shaft and help to add body to fine hair.

Try blow-drying hair using volumizing and styling products particularly focused on the roots, and tip your head upside-down as you direct airflow at the roots. You could also try self-grip rollers as they can help give you root lift (the longer the hair, the larger the roller should be).

Dull hair

Lacklustre hair can be caused by weathering – a combination of heat, salt, chlorine or silica build-up from the overuse of products.

Haircare Use a clarifying shampoo to deep-clean hair. Consider having ends trimmed and look for a revitalizing treatment to renourish hair and add condition and shine.

Static hair

Often caused by a dry atmosphere, particularly air-conditioned rooms, or hair coming into contact with synthetic materials such as nylon pillows, static is especially bad for flyaway hair, making it doubly uncontrollable.

Haircare Counter static by fixing hair in place with holding wax, gels and styling products that give the hair weight.

Frizzy hair

The merest hint of moisture being absorbed into the hair can cause frizziness. It looks dry, lacks lustre, and is difficult to control. It can also be inherited or caused by rough treatment.

Haircare To tame frizziness, massage shampoo into the roots and allow the lather to work its way to the ends. Apply a conditioner from the mid-lengths of the hair to the ends, or use a leave-in conditioner.

Alternatively, allow the hair to dry naturally and then style it using a wax or pomade. Gels with oil content and serums can also help. There are silicon-based products that work by surrounding the cuticle with a transparent microscopic film, which leaves the hair shaft smoother. Serums effectively prevent moisture loss and inhibit the absorption of dampness from the surrounding air.

Wayward curls

Messed-up curls, whether natural, on permed hair or temporarily styled, can be a pain.

Haircare Define curls more cleanly by using sculpting lotion on damp hair before setting the hair, or spritzing dry hair with curl defining spray, which gives weight and shape to tired curls.

Untrainable hair

No-hold hair which is heavy and inclined to fall out of shape.

Haircare Wayward hair can be encouraged to stay put by using a strong-hold mousse or gel spray on damp hair which is then rough-dried to about 80 per cent dry then more product applied before working that final shape. Make sure each section of hair is thoroughly dried and cooled into the required shape before moving on to the next.

Below *Applying a strong-hold mousse or gel spray to damp hair before drying can help tame wayward locks.*

Product build-up

This is often the residue of styling products and two-in-one shampoo formulation left on the hair shaft. When these residues combine with mineral deposits in the water, a build-up occurs, preventing thorough cleansing and conditioning. The result is dull, lacklustre, flat hair that is often difficult to perm or colour successfully because there is a barrier preventing the chemicals from penetrating the hair shaft. The colour can be patchy and the perm result uneven.

Haircare Use a stripping, chelating or clarifying shampoo, as these are specially designed to remove product build-up. This is particularly important prior to perming or colouring as it may affect the process.

Discoloured hair

Hair that is discoloured or even green can be caused by the blue dye that is used to show up the chlorine in swimming pools. Highlighted or porous hair will pick up the dye, which is absorbed into the hair shaft.

Haircare Try a detox shampoo or even concentrated tomato juice or ketchup as the red colouring neutralizes the green tinge. A hairdresser can usually help if the problem persists. Swimmers can also buy special shampoos and try wearing a swimming cap.

Below *Wearing a cap when swimming will help prevent lighter hair from becoming discoloured by chlorine.*

Above *Although styling products are key to good-looking hair, they can result in build-up.*

Misuse of hairdryers

An itchy or tight scalp may be an indication of a condition developing that needs treating, but it may simply be that you are overheating your head and causing skin to dry out and become irritated.

Haircare Try using slightly cooler water during your cleansing and conditioning routine. Hold hairdryers further away from your head (15cm/6in is ideal) and use heat-protective sprays before heat styling, as they protect the hair and the scalp from scorching. Try changing your haircare and styling products for more gentle ones. Check out new calming and soothing serums for the scalp, which are available to apply during the day or overnight. If the problem persists, seek further help.

Quick fixes for when time is short

- To revive or add volume to tired hair when there is not time to wash it, spritz the roots with blow-drying spray, then dry the hair, focusing on the roots.
- Revive naturally curly hair by spritzing with water and twisting into ringlets using your fingers.
- Wake up flat hair by tipping your head upside down and spraying the roots with hairspray – not too much or your hair will feel sticky and overloaded.
- When pinning up hair, lightly backcomb the roots to add guts and something for the pins to grip on to.

Trichoptilosis (split ends)

When hairs split at their ends it is often a sign of hair that is past its best.
Haircare The hair should be well-oiled to soften and remoisturize the dry ends. It's not possible to mend the splits – they will need to be trimmed – but applying split-end treatments may temporarily ease their unsightly appearance.

Hypertrichosis (excess hair)

This is where there is superfluous hair, or an abnormal development of hair on any area of the body where you would usually expect to find only downy hair.
Haircare This unwanted hair can be removed by tweezers or depilatory products, electrolysis, shaving or epilation, either in a salon, clinic or at home.

Trichotillomania (hair-pulling)

This is a condition when someone feels compelled to pull their hair out, usually on their scalp, perhaps in the same place, or even their eyebrows and eyelashes.
Haircare Sufferers can usually be helped through counselling, hypnosis or even drug therapies.

Alopecia (hair loss) or baldness

This is the technical term for any type of abnormal hair loss, in other words where the hair is shed and not replaced.

Diet, stress, pollution, illness and medication, and genetic factors come into play, and may have caused the hair follicle to become damaged and stop producing keratin. It may be that hormone treatments and better nutrition and mineral supplements can help slow down or halt further loss. It is also caused by medication or treatments such as chemotherapy, in which case the condition is often reversed when the treatment stops. Some of the most common types include:

- **Alopecia senilis** is the common form of baldness that occurs in old age. It is not permanent.
- **Alopecia premature** is a form of baldness that begins before middle age. The hair is shed gradually and replaced by thinner, weaker hair.
- **Traction alopecia** is when hair is physically stressed by being pulled back too tightly, for example into a ponytail.
- **Alopecia areata** is where patches of hair fall out for no apparent reason or due to injury to the nervous system. It's often associated with auto-immune disorders. Affected areas are smooth, slightly depressed and pale in colour due to decreased blood supply. Treatments and drug therapies can help. You will need to consult a doctor or trichologist.
- **Post-partum alopecia** occurs after having a baby and breast-feeding, when hormonal inbalances cause more hair than usual to fall out. While worrying, this usually corrects itself within months.
- **Alopecia totalis** is the total loss of scalp and facial hair. Hair does not normally regrow and you will need to consult a doctor or trichologist.
- **Alopecia universalis** is the total loss of all hair from the body and scalp. It can be caused by a major shock or an accident, and regrowth is rare. You will need to consult a doctor or trichologist.

Flaky/itchy scalp

This condition produces tiny white pieces of dead skin that flake off the scalp and are usually first noticed on the shoulders. It can often be confused with dandruff but the two are not related. Sometimes the scalp is red or itchy and feels tense.

The cause could be hereditary traits, stress, insufficient rinsing of shampoo, lack of sebum, using too harsh a shampoo, vitamin imbalance, pollution, air-conditioning and central heating, and sometimes it is a side-effect of medication, including chemotherapy.
Haircare Calming serums and lotions are available (some intended to be used at night-time) and are a soothing way to tackle the problem and remoisturize the scalp. Ask a trichologist or hair salon for advice on these and on how to address the cause with improved haircare regimes and diet.

Dandruff

This happens when scaly particles with an oily sheen lie close to the hair root. The condition should not be confused with a flaky scalp, and is nothing to do with poor hygiene or stress. Causes are thought to be a microscopic fungal yeast called *Malassezia furfur*, which is present in everyone's scalp. Sometimes, when the scalp becomes irritated, skin cells produce greater amounts of the yeast, causing cells to clump together and

Below *Hair loss caused by medical treatments such as chemotherapy should be temporary.*

Below *Pulling hair too tight on a regular basis can cause traction alopecia.*

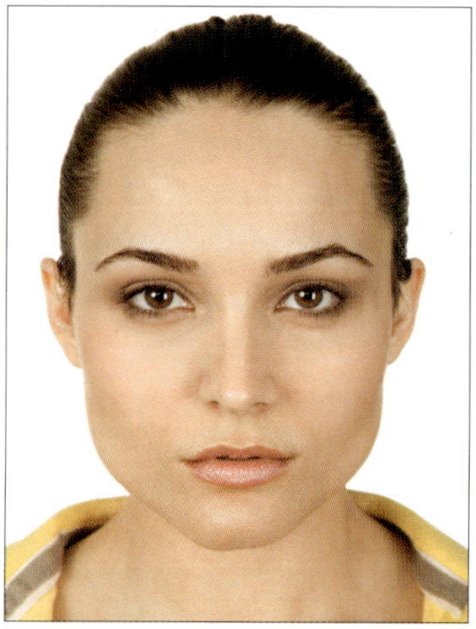

produce flakes of dandruff. A poor diet, sluggish metabolism, and a hormonal imbalance can make things worse. It may be that insufficient rinsing of the hair after shampooing, or the use of strong shampoos also contributes to dandruff.
Haircare Don't necessarily rush out to buy special treatment shampoos. They may be beneficial, but it's worth thinking longer term by looking at your diet and lifestyle. You could try brushing the hair before shampooing and scrupulously washing combs and hairbrushes. Always choose a mild shampoo and perhaps a moisturizing one. Avoid excessive use of heat stylers. If the dandruff persists, try specially labelled products or consult a doctor or trichologist.

Psoriasis

This condition can affect the entire scalp or just the hairline. It is typified by raised red patches covered with silvery-white scales, which can be itchy, tight and sore. It is caused by excessive skin production.
Haircare Herbal or aromatherapy products may help but it is best to consult a doctor or trichologist, who may be able to prescribe a range of treatments.

Eczema

This skin condition is typified by tight, dry and irritated skin that can become broken and sore.
Haircare It's important to use very mild cleansing products, or simply rinse hair in water if skin is irritated by soap and shampoos. Comb very gently to avoid exacerbating the problem further.

Seborrhoeic dermatitis

This is a non-infectious type of skin inflammation caused by the same fungal yeast that is responsible for dandruff. It can be aggravated by stress, or even inherited. In babies the condition is commonly called cradle cap. The tell-tale signs are large, greasy, yellowish scales that stick to the scalp; inflammation of the skin and mild patches of flaky skin on the face. In extreme cases, a rash of red, scaly skin can develop on the scalp and face.

Above *Dandruff is unsightly but not something to worry about too much. Vigorous brushing before washing may help.*

Haircare An anti-dandruff shampoo should help but, if not, consult a doctor or trichologist.

Sebaceous cysts

These are marble-like lumps that occur when keratin accumulates under the skin and forms single bumps or clusters of several at a time. There are not normally painful but may be big enough to catch on a hairbrush or comb.
Haircare They may need removing, so consult a doctor or trichologist.

Infection

Easily spread, infections are caused by harmful germs and bacteria. They are contagious and must be treated, and will affect the condition of the scalp and hair.

- **Bacterial infections**, such as boils and impetigo, can be treated with antibiotics. Viruses survive in all living cells of the body, so colds and flu will affect hair condition, too.
- **Fungal infections** will feed on keratin and can spread to the scalp. They include ringworm, so must be treated quickly or they may cause hair loss.

Above *Regularly washing combs and brushes can help prevent problems such as dandruff, keeping your hair in superb condition.*

Infestation

It's an uncomfortable fact of life that from time to time hair may become infested with lice, which transfer from head to head through direct contact. Lice often spread rapidly between children who will lean in close to each other at school or play, but equally affect adults, so it's very important to be aware of the possibility of lice transferring to other family members.

The lice lay eggs (called nits), which are very hard to dislodge. Because they need warm temperatures, the lice or nits will be found closer to the scalp rather than down the hair. They cling tenaciously to the hair shaft.
Haircare Nits and lice will literally have to be combed out using a special fine-toothed comb most commonly found at pharmacists. It's possible to buy chemical formulations, which manufacturers claim kill the lice, but their efficiency is debatable, and regular combing to both remove lice and keep further attacks at bay is highly recommended. Once the lice or nits are removed, comb the hair with a fine comb a minimum of once every three days, sterilizing the comb between uses.

Shampooing hair

Establishing an efficient and effective haircare routine starts with great cleansing. Depending on whether you are washing daily or several times a week, and on the type and needs of your hair, there are several guides you can follow.

Why shampoo?

Designed to cleanse the hair and scalp, shampoos remove dirt without stripping away too much of the natural sebum, which provides shine. They generally contain cleansing agents, perfume, preservatives and conditioning agents that can coat the hair shaft to make it appear thicker. The conditioning agents smooth the cuticle scales to help prevent the hair from tangling and eliminate static electricity from the hair when it dries.

Different types of shampoo

There is a huge range of shampoos (some of which are called cleansers or hairbaths), so it's possible to find one suited to every hair type, texture, colour or condition. It is important that you change your shampoo according to different circumstances. For example, in the summer, use a moisturizing shampoo with a sun protection factor; when colouring, use a product to help prevent colour fade; or when suffering a condition such as dandruff, opt for a specialist type.

The pH factor

This refers to the acid/alkaline level of a substance. It is calculated on a scale of 1 to 14. Numbers below 7 denote acidity, those over 7 indicate alkalinity.

Hair sebum has a pH factor of between 4.5 and 5.5, which is mildly acidic. Bacteria cannot survive in this pH, so it is important to maintain this protective layer of sebum in order to keep the skin, scalp and hair in optimum condition. If too acidic or too alkaline a product is used on hair, it may cause hair to become porous, weakened and even break.

Most shampoos range between a pH factor of 5 and 7; medicated varieties have a pH of about 7.3, which is near neutral.

Many shampoos are labelled 'pH balanced', and restore hair to its natural acidity, which is especially useful after chemical treatments such as colouring.

Scalp massage

Massage helps maintain a healthy scalp. It brings extra blood to the skin tissue, which enhances the delivery of nutrients and oxygen to the hair follicle. Massage also reduces scalp tension – which can contribute to hair loss – loosens dead skin cells, and perhaps helps redress the overproduction of sebum, which makes hair oily.

You can easily give yourself a scalp massage at home. Use warm olive oil if the scalp is dry or tight. Try equal parts of witch hazel and mineral water if you have an oily scalp. For a normal scalp, use equal parts rose and mineral waters. Simply warm the chosen ointment in your hands, apply to the scalp evenly, then

Left *Once you have established a routine that suits your hair type and current condition, it can be quick and easy to maintain.*

Above *Just as you would alter your facial cleanser to suit your skin type, select a shampoo according to your current needs.*

begin massaging your scalp at the hairline and work backwards to the base of your skull. Once you have reached the back, start again at your temples and work backwards. Use small, circular motions and medium pressure.

Tips for shampooing

- Use the correct shampoo (and not too much) for your hair type. If in doubt, use the mildest shampoo you can buy.
- Don't wash your hair in washing-up liquid, soap or other detergents; they are highly alkaline and will upset your hair's pH balance by stripping out the natural oils.
- Read the instructions for use first as every product varies slightly.
- Buy sachets of shampoo to test which brand is the most suitable for your hair.
- Never wash your hair in the bath; dirty bath water is not conducive to clean hair.
- Always wash your hairbrush and comb when you shampoo your hair.
- Don't throw away a shampoo that doesn't lather. The amount of suds is determined by the active level of detergent and some shampoos create less suds than others, but this has no effect on their cleansing ability.

Did you know?

Most of us don't spend enough time rinsing off shampoo – it really should be a step that takes at least two minutes. Avoid using water that is too hot as it may irritate and inflame the scalp.

Shampooing hair

Taking care of healthy hair starts with a great cleansing routine. It's not rocket science but there is a technique to follow that means you will maintain maximum condition for scalp and hair.

1 Wet hair thoroughly using a shower, ensuring all the layers are completely soaked through – this will activate the shampoo properly when it is applied.

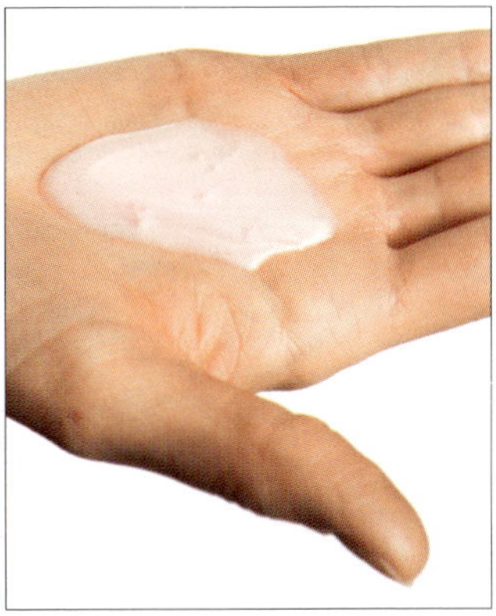

2 Pour the shampoo into the palm of your hand, never directly on to the hair as it's tricky to control how much you use. For short hair you only need the same amount as a small coin, for longer hair you may require more, but never more than you can easily hold in the palm of your hand.

3 Work the shampoo through the hair, massaging your scalp and paying particular attention to the hairline around the ears and base of the neck. It should lather well but not too much.

4 Rinse away all the shampoo, then pat hair dry or squeeze gently to get rid of excess water. Don't rub or you will cause hair to tangle or break. Wet hair is more vulnerable than dry hair.

Conditioning hair

Hair in good condition is manageable, shiny, flexible and feels soft. Ideally, a simple shampoo would guarantee gorgeous results, but conditioning is often required to combat stresses caused by chemical processes, as well as to rectify problems.

Why condition?

Glossy hair has cuticle scales that lie flat and overlap, reflecting light. Perming and colouring, rough handling and heat-styling all conspire to lift the cuticles and roughen them up, both allowing moisture to be lost from the cortex and making hair dry, lacklustre, and prone to tangle. Severely damaged cuticles break off completely, leaving the hair's cortex exposed, which leads to splits and breakages.

To put the shine back into hair and restore its natural lustre it may be necessary to use a specific conditioner that meets your hair's requirements. Conditioners, with the exception of hot oils, should be applied to freshly-shampooed hair that has been blotted dry with a towel so that it is damp rather than wet.

Different types of conditioners

Conditioning products are delivered in different formats and have different effects:

- **Basic conditioners** coat the hair with a fine film, temporarily smoothing down the cuticle and making hair glossier and easier to manage. Leave on the hair for a few minutes before rinsing thoroughly.
- **Leave-in conditioners**, in spray or cream format, are intended to be applied after cleansing hair. Follow the instructions on the bottle, then leave on the hair when drying and styling. They save time and are perfect for limited use when hair is extra-dry, after colouring, or when intense heat is used.

Below left *Heavier masques and crème treatments can be used on a once-a-week basis to restore hair's condition.*

Below *Hair that is well-conditioned should feel soft, flexible and be easy to manage.*

- **Conditioning sprays** are designed to be used prior to styling and form a protective barrier against the harmful effects of heat. They are also good for reducing static electricity on flyaway hair.
- **Hot oils** give an intensive, deep nourishing treatment. To use, place the unopened tube in a cup of hot tap water and leave to heat for one minute. Next, wet the hair and towel it dry before twisting off the tube top. Massage the hot oil evenly into the scalp and throughout the hair for one to three minutes. For a more intensive treatment, cover the head with a shower cap and leave to penetrate. To finish, rinse the hair, then shampoo.
- **Intensive conditioning treatments** can be applied both in a salon – often as part of a ritual or service – or for occasional use at home. They may be rich crèmes or masques, and using them will help hair to retain its natural moisture balance, replenishing it where necessary. Use particularly if the hair is split, dry, frizzy, or difficult to manage.
- **Restructurants** penetrate the cortex, helping to repair and strengthen the inner part of damaged hair. They are helpful if the hair is lank and limp and has lost its natural elasticity as a result of chemical treatments or physical damage.
- **Split-end treatments and serums** condition damaged hair. The best course of action for split ends is to have the ends trimmed, but this does not always solve the whole problem because the hair tends to break off and split at different levels. As an intermediate solution, split ends can appear to be temporarily sealed using these specialist conditioners.
- **Colour/perm conditioners** are designed for chemically-treated hair. After-colour products add a protective film around porous areas of the hair, preventing colour loss. After-perm products help stabilize the hair, thus keeping the bounce in the curl.

Did you know?

If you find your hair becomes oilier more quickly than usual, it may be that your conditioner is too heavy. Don't immediately discard it, rather try rinsing if off sooner than usual, and perhaps applying less.

Conditioning hair

Most hair that has been treated with a chemical process or exposed to environmental stresses will need either regular or occasional conditioning treatments after shampooing. Be careful not to apply too much conditioner – a little is designed to go a long way, and using too much product will make the hair feel lank and weighed down.

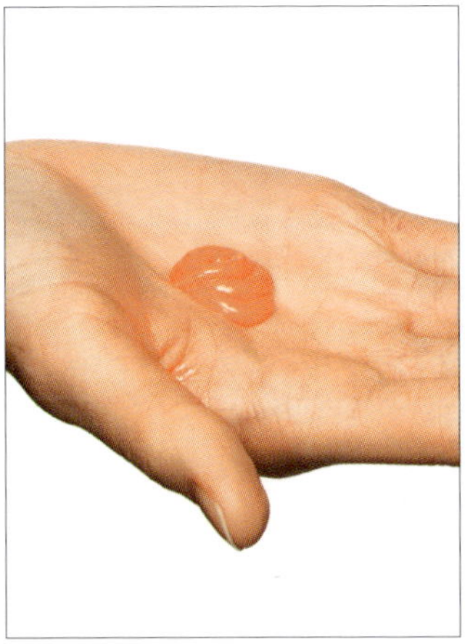

1 Follow the instructions on the packaging, but as a general guide, use only a large coin-sized amount of product on mid-length hair, and less on shorter hair.

2 Rub the product lightly over the palms of both hands to make it easier to apply, then distribute it evenly along the lengths of damp (not soaking wet), cleansed hair.

3 Work the product through the mid-lengths and ends rather than trying to massage it into the scalp, which is not usually necessary since the root area is new growth, which should be in a good condition naturally. Comb through hair gently using a wide-tooth comb to ensure the conditioner is evenly distributed. This type of comb is less likely to pull and break hair than other smaller-toothed combs. The conditioner should make it easy to detangle the hair. Wait the indicated amount of time (usually 2–5 minutes) to allow the conditioner to penetrate, before rinsing off with warm water. Towel dry, then comb again.

Natural treatments

In cultures the world over, herbs and plants have been used to heal and beautify. Many of these age-old haircare recipes are still useful today and you may find them worth a try. Use them immediately after you have made them; they won't keep.

Herbal shampoo

Crush a few dried bay leaves with a rolling pin and mix with a handful of dried camomile flowers and one handful of rosemary. Place in a large jug and pour over 1 litre/1¾ pints/4 cups boiling water. Strain after 2–3 minutes and mix in 5ml/1 tsp of soft or liquid soap. Apply to the hair, massaging well for a minute or two. Rinse thoroughly.

For condition and shine:

- **Egg mask** Blend two eggs with 30ml/2 tbsp water and 15ml/1 tbsp cider vinegar or lemon juice. Massage into damp hair and leave for 10–15 minutes before rinsing thoroughly with lukewarm (not hot) water.
- **Banana mask** Mix together 1 mashed banana, 45ml/3 tbsp honey, 45ml/3 tbsp milk, 75ml/5 tbsp olive oil and 1 egg. Apply to damp hair and massage so it is evenly distributed. Leave on the hair for up to 30 minutes, then rinse thoroughly and shampoo and condition your hair as usual.
- **Yogurt mask** Prepare by blending 105ml/7 tbsp plain (natural) yogurt with the beaten white of 1 egg. Apply to damp hair, massage through the roots to ends and leave for up to 30 minutes. Shampoo and condition your hair as usual.
- **Avocado, honey and olive oil** are also great hair conditioners. You can use them in different combinations (olive oil whisked with egg, or honey and olive oil blended in equal parts) or all together. Simply conjure up a consistency to suit you, leave on as long as you like to work their magic, and then shampoo and rinse hair well.

Rinses (after shampooing)

Lemon juice added to the rinsing water will brighten blonde hair, while 30ml/2 tbsp of cider vinegar will add gloss and body to any colour hair.

Other rinses (to be used after shampooing) can be made up to treat a variety of problems. First you must make an infusion by placing 30ml/2 tbsp of a fresh herb in a china or glass bowl. Fresh herbs are best, but if you are using dried ones, remember they are stronger so you will need to halve the amount required for fresh herbs. Add 600ml/1 pint boiling water, cover and leave to steep for three hours. Strain before using. Try:

- **Southernwood** to combat oiliness.
- **Nettle** to stimulate hair growth.
- **Rosemary** to prevent static.
- **Lavender** to soothe a tight scalp.
- **Tea tree** to ward off infestation.

Left *Banana and avocado fruit make nourishing hair masks.*

Using essential oils

Pure aromatherapy oils can be used for hair care. The following recipes come from world-famous aromatherapist Robert Tisserand. The number of drops of oil, as listed, should be diluted in 30ml/2 tbsp (or two large spoons) of vegetable oil, which will act as a carrier oil:

- **Dry hair**: rosewood 9, sandalwood 6.
- **Oily hair**: bergamot 9, lavender 6.
- **Dandruff**: eucalyptus 9, rosemary 6.

Mix the required treatment and apply to dry or wet hair. Massage the scalp using the fingertips. Leave for 2–5 minutes. Shampoo and rinse thoroughly.

Left *Let natural essential oils work their magic, restoring hair condition, shine and vitality and combating dandruff.*

Happy holidays

More damage can be done to hair during a two-week holiday in the sun than over the rest of the year! To ensure your hair enjoys the break as much as you do, it is important that you prepare well and pack products to keep you looking perfect all holiday long.

Almost every aspect of a holiday in the sun can wreak havoc on our hair. The ultraviolet rays or radiation (UVRs) from sunlight that can cause damage to the skin also have an adverse affect on hair, depleting it of natural oils and removing moisture. White hair is particularly susceptible to the effects of the sun because it has lost its natural pigmentation (melanin), which would normally help to filter out harmful UVRs to a certain extent.

Exposure to strong winds can whip treated hair into a tangle, causing breakage and split ends, while chlorinated and salt water cause colour to fade and treated hair to weaken and dry out substantially faster than untreated hair. As if that wasn't bad enough, chlorine can also cause blonde, grey or white hair to take on a greenish tinge.

Sun and wind protection

Protecting your hair as well as your skin from the sun's harmful rays makes sense. This can be done by wearing a hat or a scarf and using a specially formulated product. Sunscreen sprays and gels are available for the hair and these offer a good deal of protection. Comb them through your hair and leave on all day. Remember to reapply the product after swimming. Alternatively, use a leave-in conditioner, choosing one that protects the hair against UVRs.

On windy or blustery days, keep long hair tied back to prevent tangles. Long hair can also be plaited (braided) when it is wet and the plait left in all day, which offers some protection. When evening comes and you undo the plaits, you will have a cascade of rippling curls.

Below *Be kind to your hair and make sure your two-week holiday isn't going to leave you with problem hair for the rest of the season.*

If your hair does get tangled by the wind, untangle it gently using a wide-tooth comb to reduce risk of tearing and snagging, and spritz hair with conditioning spray to ease the combing process.

Holiday care

You may want to wash your hair more often than normal while on holiday. Generally speaking, you should always wash it at least once a day if you have been in a swimming pool or on the beach to get rid of salt, chlorine and sand build-up. This is perfectly fine and, contrary to the popular myth, won't mean that your hair becomes oilier and requires more washing on your return home. Even if you don't shampoo hair every time, always rinse the salt or chlorinated water thoroughly from hair after a swim, using plenty of fresh, clean water. If there is no shower, fill an empty bottle with tap water and use that instead.

Natural highlights

Exposure to the sun will fade your hair colour and make it appear lightened, which many people like. But remember this is a drying action, so you will need to replace lost moisture with conditioner. Too much sun can also burn the scalp. Applying lemon juice to speed up the lightening process is not advised, as not only is there debate over its effectiveness, but the natural citric acid can be damaging.

Pre-trip action

- Any hair colouring you are planning should be done at least one week prior to your holiday. This will allow time for the colour to 'soften' and for you to apply intensive conditioning on any dry ends.
- If you want to have a perm, book the appointment at least three weeks before departure to allow hair to settle and for you to learn how to manage your new style.

Above right *It is vital that you wash, or at least rinse your hair after swimming in the sea or in a swimming pool.*

Right *A sun hat and a few sun-protection products, including a bottle of water, are must-haves for trips to the beach.*

▪ Have your hair trimmed before you go, but do not try a radical style as you won't want to worry about coping with a new look. Whatever you do, don't have your hair cut abroad. Wait until you are back home and can visit your regular stylist.

On the beach

Exposed to sun, sand, and salt or chlorinated water, your hair will require a little extra care. Here are a few top tips:

▪ Tie hair at the nape of the neck rather then piling it on top of your head. This protects the ends from over-exposure to the sun.

▪ Take a bottle of tap water to the beach so you can rinse salt water out of your hair during the day.

▪ Reapply hair protection during the day as often as you would body protection. One spritz in the morning is not enough.

▪ Use covered hairbands (headbands) to tie back hair. Keep a scarf handy to tie hair back and cover it up in emergencies.

▪ In small quantities, you can use skin-protection body lotions or sprays on the hair and scalp.

On the piste

Although we may not realize it, cold temperatures, wind and reflected winter sunlight can be just as damaging to hair as beach conditions. It is important to follow these basic rules:

▪ The sun's rays are intensified by being reflected by snow, so hair needs extra protection in the form of a hair sunscreen.

▪ Wind, blasts of snow, and bright sunshine are a damaging combination for hair, so wear a hat whenever possible.

▪ In freezing temperatures hair picks up static electricity, making it flyaway and unmanageable. Calm the static by spraying your hairbrush with hairspray before brushing your hair.

▪ With sudden temperature changes and constantly changing headgear, your hair may need daily shampooing. Use a mild shampoo and light conditioner.

Right *A hat is the best way to protect hair from environmental stresses, such as cold and glare from the sun bouncing off snow.*

Back home

Your holiday is over, but while a tan fades quickly, the negative effects it has had on your hair may be noticeable for some time to come. Here are some easy ways to combat the more common problems:

▪ Use a clarifying shampoo or treatment to remove deep deposits of dirt and build-up of holiday styling products. Remember to stop using it, however, once hair is back in condition.

▪ Dry or flaky scalp often occurs due to over-exposure to sun, sand and wind. Applying an intensive deep-conditioning treatment that includes a scalp treatment to rehydrate the skin will help.

▪ Book in for a trim to get rid of over-dry or split ends.

▪ When on holiday it's tempting to over-indulge in a little too much food and wine, and your diet may vary quite a bit from what your body is used to. Just like your skin, your hair will be affected, so once home, calm things down with a detox diet!

▪ If you have acquired a greenish tinge (lightened hair is most at risk), then a detoxifying shampoo should help. Or, try applying concentrated tomato juice or ketchup to the hair as the red colouring should neutralize any green. If it won't budge, then visit the salon for a specialist deep-cleanse treatment.

Pack a bag

With the luxury of a large bathroom cabinet to store all the products you need to create different looks, it can be a headache deciding what to pack when you have to travel. Here are few ideas on what should be included depending on what size bag you have.

When planning a trip, you need to consider how long you are going for, what you will be doing and how much space you have in your luggage. Think through what activities and appointments you have and how you might want to style your hair. Do you need styling lotions, mousse, serums and spray? All will be available in travel sizes or you can decant them into smaller containers.

Go large

If room isn't a major factor but weight is, then just include the following products and equipment:

- Appropriate-sized bottles and tubs of your favourite shampoo and conditioner.
- Moisturizing conditioning treatment for use once or twice a week on a long trip. You can opt for vials or sachets rather than a large pot when you only plan to use a small amount.
- Detox shampoo to combat a change of environment, including heat, dust, or smog.
- Dry shampoo for whenever you don't have time to follow your normal routine.
- Nearly finished canisters of mousse, spray and gel are great for travel as you can use them up and discard them.
- Covered hairbands (headbands) or hair slides (barrettes) are ideal for tying hair back, whatever the occasion.
- Combs, including a wide-tooth comb.
- A large, round brush for smooth, sleek styling or creating flicks and curl.
- If possible, take a travel hairdryer with dual voltage.
- Pack an adaptor plug suitable for the country you are visiting.
- If you're travelling to somewhere hotter or colder than you are used to, take a scarf and a hat for ultimate protection. Sun hats in cotton can be folded small and woolly ski hats are a fun style statement.
- Battery or gas-powered stylers are now widely available in a range of sizes and are convenient for holidays, but remember they must be carried in the hold of the aircraft, not in your hand luggage. Refill cylinders are not allowed on aeroplanes, so make sure you fit a new cartridge before you go.
- Soft, bendy rods or self-grip rollers are a good alternative to heated ones – they are also kinder to the hair.

***Right** You can buy miniature versions of many hair-styling products, or buy small, empty containers and fill them yourself.*

Medium size

If you need to travel a little lighter, then here are some easy ideas for condensing the essentials:

- Sachets of products – shampoo and conditioner, styling lotion – are perfect for travelling. Not only do they squash flat with no fear of leaking, but you can discard them as you go.
- A small tub of talcum powder can double as dry shampoo.
- Hairbands (headbands) and hairgrips (bobby pins) are small, very useful and easy to pack.
- Combs, including a wide-tooth comb, are always required.
- It is worth calling where you are staying to check if a hairdryer will be supplied.
- Mini straightening irons (even handbag irons are available) not only heat quickly but take little room. You can pep up fringes and flicks in no time.
- Self-grip rollers are bulky but light and can prove valuable if your hair goes limp.
- A scarf can protect hair and be a stylish accessory for a range of occasions. A silk scarf can also be wrapped around hair at night to reduce static if hotel pillows and air-conditioning are creating static and frizz.

Left A good way to disguise oily hair when you don't have time to wash it and don't have dry shampoo is apply talcum powder on to the roots, then brush it out.

Travelling light

When you are very short of space or only going away for couple of nights, it's possible to create a neat haircare kit that contains all the vitals for cool styles:

- Two-in-one shampoo and conditioners are available in small travel sizes or sachets, which you can discard as you go. In the short-term, it's fine to use them on a daily basis. (After prolonged use they can cause product build-up, so only use them for a few days.)
- A small bottle or tube of serum multi-tasks as a quick way to calm flyaways, smooth out frizz and add instant shine.
- Take a miniature styling spray, which can be used for hold, to pep-up tired hair by spritzing the roots, or as a protector against heat- and wind-stress.
- Take enough matt hairgrips (bobby pins) to fix a chignon or up-do, both of which are great ways of dealing with 'day-old' hair. Matt rather than shiny ones won't show so much and will grip better.
- Covered hairbands (headbands) are invaluable – when all else fails, tie your hair back!
- Always include a hairbrush and/or comb.

Must-haves

Although you can get by without many products, most hair types do require a few basic help-out items:

- **Coloured hair** can fade in sunlight, so pack products to prevent or limit colour fade and keep you looking fabulous. Cold weather and wind can be very drying and make hair brittle, so keep your hair well-conditioned.
- **Fine hair** requires a gentle daily shampoo and a light, leave-in conditioner. Hairsprays are also needed to hold down the cuticle of the hair and keep out moisture in humid conditions and reduce static in cold environments.
- **Curly hair** needs a gentle moisturizing shampoo and creamy conditioner to guard against dryness from sun or air-conditioning, plus a deep-conditioning treatment for occasional use.
- **Frizzy hair** benefits from a sun- or heat-protection spray or oil, a hair mask for intensive treatment if the hair becomes too dry, and a good anti-frizz serum to calm hair and lock in moisture whatever the weather.

Double-ups

Sometimes, despite the best planning, you may forget something. There's often no need rush out to buy a replacement, however, simply see if you can use one of our clever subsitutes instead:

- **No dry shampoo?** Tip talcum powder on to the roots of your hair where it will absorb any excess oil, then brush it out thoroughly. Dabbing witch hazel on to roots will also absorb any oil. Both these techniques will work for one day, but you will then need to shampoo your hair properly.

Left and above *Lightweight rollers and covered hairbands (headbands) are an essential part of a savvy stylist's washbag.*

Above *When space is limited, rationalizing the contents of your washbag will mean you are never less than prepared!*

- **No conditioner?** See if you can get an avocado, some honey or some oil! Blend the ingredients (mashing up the avocado) and work the mixture into damp, clean hair. Leave it to penetrate for a few minutes, then shampoo and rinse off thoroughly.
- **No serum?** Leave-in conditioner can be applied to the ends of the hair like serum to smooth and remoisturize dry ends. Hairspray will also calm flyaways and reduce frizz.
- **No heat-protector spray?** Sun-protection body lotions and oils can be applied to the hair (don't use too much) to protect your scalp and hair from the sun. Make sure they have a suitable sun protection factor (SPF).
- **No rollers?** Firm-hold mousse can be used to create curl. Apply all over damp hair, then take small sections and twist them from roots to ends. Dry slowly using a diffuser attachment on the hairdryer or leave hair to dry naturally.
- **No tongs?** Braid damp hair and leave it to dry for as long as possible – overnight if you want – to create waves and gentle curl. The tighter the braid, the tighter the curl.
- **No accessories or ornaments?** Use jewellery to add a little fun to holiday hair. Drape lightweight bracelets or charms into the hair and secure the ends with hairgrips (bobby pins), or use a brooch to double as a hair ornament.

Successful styling

Choosing a hairstyle that suits your looks and your lifestyle means considering several factors, from the cut and styling it involves to the colour and chemical treatments that may be needed. Having achieved the perfect style, you also need to learn how to maintain it and ensure a fabulous finish every time. Today, there are many styling products and tools to help, but so much choice can be overwhelming. The trick is not only to figure out what to use and when, but how they work for you in particular, given your hair type and texture. Follow our guide and have fun!

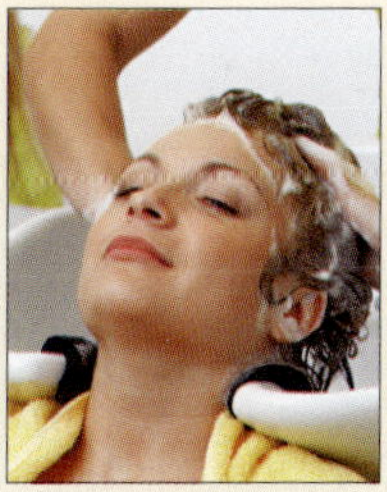

New style, new you

Looking for a new style? Fantastic. A fresh cut, colour or restyle is a great way to revamp your look and boost your confidence. However, it is important that you put some thought into what you want to achieve before you arrive at the salon.

For many women, a dramatic change – such as going from long to short, straight to curly, or brunette to blonde – coincides with a big life change, perhaps the end of a relationship or new job. It's a form of liberation and can be a great springboard into a dynamic new attitude. But be wary of making drastic decisions if you are less than 100 per cent certain. Your bravado today could be your misery tomorrow, as many changes take months to grow out and are not easily reversed.

If there's any chance you might regret your actions then go for a change with fewer commitments, such as restyling hair to include a fringe (bangs) or opting to lift or darken hair colour several tones rather than going for a complete change.

A look for a lifestyle

When browsing the pictures in this book and in magazines, think about which looks suit your age and stage. A trend can be adopted completely, or your hairdresser can incorporate an aspect of a popular look into a style – maybe a fringe detail, a colour, or texture.

Think about how much time you are prepared to spend on styling each day and whether you have the capability to maintain an elaborate look yourself. If you play sports or swim, then will daily washing and restyling require more time than you have to spare? Being a busy mum or working away a lot could also make some looks too high maintenance for your lifestyle.

Above left *It is well worth flicking through fashion magazines and the galleries in this book to help you decide what style you want.*

Left *Lifestyle activities may dictate how long or short your hair needs to be. If you do a lot of sport, you will need to wear it tied back.*

Caution pays

There are a few imaginative ways to try out a new look before you sign up for the real deal. Wanting to go from long to short? Pop on a wig or two to see how it feels. Similarly, if you want a dramatically different new colour, try a temporary hair piece in the new hue to see how it suits. A perm can be 'tried out' by getting your hair wrapped in heated rollers or bendie rods for a practice run. A good hair salon will be able to advise you not only on how a cut might suit you, but also how different hair colours will look against your skin tone.

Versatility

Talk to your hairdresser about different ways you will (or won't) be able to style your new look to suit your lifestyle, both at work and play. Will you still be able to draw hair into a ponytail for going to the gym? Can you style a new short look to be smooth or textured? How will you wear this new look for smart daytime events, or glamorous evenings out?

Thinking ahead

It's important to plan where this new hairstyle will take you. If you fancy having a short crop, then consider how long it will take to grow out and what styles you might prefer in the future. It could make sense to go for a short one-length bob that grows out quite quickly rather than a close-cut, gamine style that will take longer to move into something else.

What about colour? Adopting a new block colour will mean regrowth coming through more obviously – so consider if you have the budget to continue having roots touched up, or whether highlights are a more practical way for you to change colour without breaking the bank.

If you really want a new look that requires more hair length or volume than you currently have, then discuss with your hairdresser ways that you can work towards achieving that look in a few months time. If you hanker after one-length hair, or hate your fringe, then growing out steep layers can take up to 12 months, but it's possible to have styles and cuts in the meantime that won't compromise your end goal.

Above *Consider how versatile a new look will be – taking you from day to night, for example.*

When looking for a new style remember to consider:

- Why are you doing it? Is this really something you want to commit to?
- Do you have the right texture, volume and length of hair to achieve your desired style? In-salon consultations are free and talking with a hairdresser will give you a realistic perspective on what is possible for your hair and what could suit you best.
- Are you going to need a new wardrobe to complement a new colour, or hair length?
- How much styling time will your new look require and are you prepared to invest?
- Get inspiration from looking at others around you, friends, magazines and celebrities. Remember, however, to think about how that style will look on you; don't be dazzled solely by how it looks on them.
- Where will this new style take you? If you've spent the past couple of years trying to grow out a fringe, then will this new style put you right back where you started, or is it halfway to the next look?

Choosing a style

When it comes to choosing the perfect style, there are plenty of easy-to-follow guidelines on what cut best suits which face-shape, hair texture and type. But for all the advice, really the only rule is that you must feel confident and happy in yourself.

Fashions come and go with different trends and ideas, but essentially, if you learn to make the most of your looks by choosing a style that maximizes your best features, you will exude vitality and vigour and look beautiful because of it.

Face shapes

Understanding your face shape will help get you started. Is your face round, oval, square, heart-shaped or long? By defining your face shape and working with your stylist on a cut and style, you can minimize or emphasize different aspects of a face. Effects could include opening up the face and making the best of small eyes, revealing a great eyebrow shape, softening a strong jaw-line or giving the illusion of shortening a long chin.

If you are not sure what shape your face is, then the easiest way to find out is to draw the hair back off your face. Stand squarely in front of a mirror and use a lipstick to trace the outline of your face on to the mirror. When you stand back you should be able to see into which of the following categories your face shape falls: square, round, oval, heart-shaped or oblong.

***Above** Take time to consider your face shape and which features you want to emphasize.*

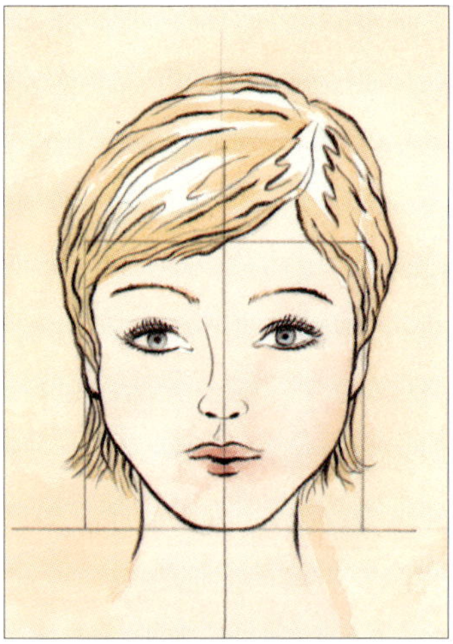

The square face is angular with a broad forehead and a square jawline. To make the best of this shape, choose a hairstyle with long layers, preferably one with gentle waves or curls, as these create a softness that detracts from the hard lines. Consider off-centre partings, loose curls and graduated cuts. Avoid blunt fringes (bangs).

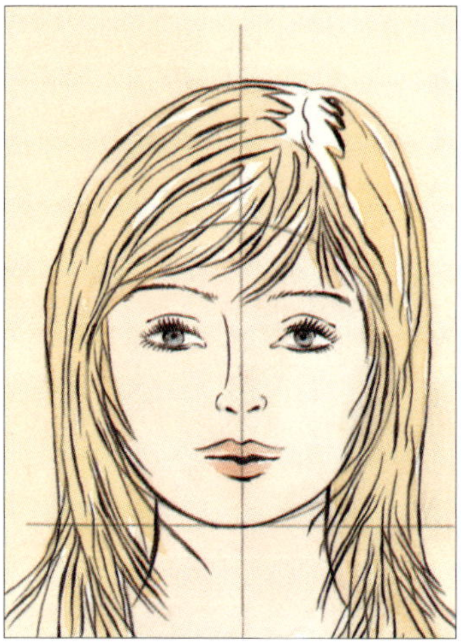

On the round face, the distance between the forehead and the chin is about equal to the distance between the cheeks. Look at feathered haircuts where the hair falls forward to slim down a fuller face. A short fringe (bangs) will seem to lengthen the face, while a shorter cut can be more flattering than a long style.

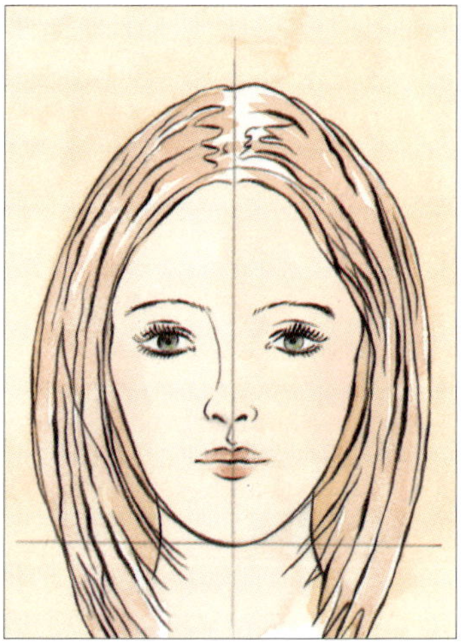

The oval face has wide cheekbones that taper down into a small, often pointed, chin, and up to a fairly narrow forehead. This is regarded by many experts as the perfect face shape, which looks good with almost any style. Now consider your facial features – do you prefer to emphasize your mouth, eyes, cheekbones or nose?

Left *A good hairstyle should match your clothes style and suit your body shape.*

The complete you

When choosing a new style you should also take into account your overall body shape and your personal lifestyle. If you are a traditional pear-shape, perhaps don't go for neat, elfin styles as they accentuate a small head shape and allow attention to be drawn to the lower half of your body, making your hips look even wider. Petite women might avoid styles with masses of very curly hair as this makes the head appear larger and out of proportion with the body.

If you wear glasses, try to choose frames and a hairstyle that complement each other. Large spectacles could spoil the look of a neat, feathery cut, while very fine frames could be overpowered by a large, voluminous style. Remember to take your glasses to the salon when having your hair restyled, so that your stylist can take their shape into consideration when helping you decide on a cut.

To minimize signs of ageing, opt for a neater, more sophisticated cut, which can knock years off your look – leaving more tousled, casual styles to younger women. Don't get stuck in a style rut. Nothing is more dating than a tired look. Re-energize yourself with a new style from time to time. It doesn't have to be drastic, but a variation on a cut or colour works wonders for your appearance and for your mood.

Feature notes

You can use hairstyles to help disguise features that you don't particularly like:

- **Prominent nose?** Incorporate softness into your style.
- **Pointed chin?** Style the hair with width at the jawline.
- **Low forehead?** Choose a style with a wispy fringe (bangs), rather than one with a full fringe.
- **High forehead?** Disguise a large forehead with a full fringe.
- **Receding chin?** Select a style that comes just below chin level, with waves or curls.
- **Uneven hairline?** A fringe should help conceal this problem.

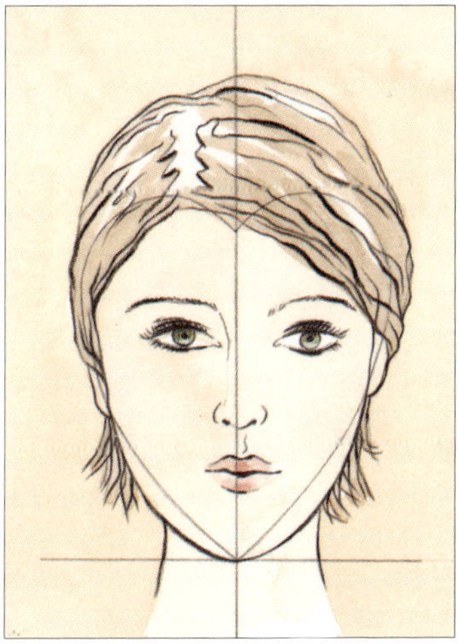

The heart-shaped face, where the widest point is at eye-level and then it tapers down to a neater chin shape, can be balanced by creating volume or width at chin level. A bob that flicks out just below the ears for example, can look fabulous. Or create volume at chin level with curls, layers or shattered perimeters.

The oblong face is characterized by a high forehead and long chin, and needs a haircut that gives the illusion of width to balance it. Soften the effect with short layers, or go for a bob with a fringe (bangs), which will create horizontal lines. Scrunch-dried or curly bobs balance a long face, too.

Choosing a hairdresser

A fantastic haircut, an eye-catching new style and gorgeous hair that is well groomed and exudes health and vitality all play a major part in how we feel, so it's important to find a hairdresser you trust to care for, cut and colour your hair.

Going to the hairdresser can be expensive, and the outcome is likely to last for a few weeks, so it's worth really taking the time to find one that suits you.

Understand your hairdresser

Hairdressers are trained to care for hair and learn how to cut, colour, style and treat it. They should also be practised in assessing which looks are best suited to which face shapes, how to assess hair types and textures, and which colours will or won't work well with different skin tones and complexions. Add to this their ability to interpret fashion trends and pass on knowledge about new products and services, and a good hairdresser is worth their weight in gold.

Before any hair appointment, you should expect a consultation with your hairdresser. The purpose of this is for them to find out what you want and to decide on a safe, appropriate and effective service to ensure you get the perfect result.

Choose a salon

Word of mouth is often the best way to select a new salon. Ask around, particularly friends or acquaintances whose hair you admire (they'll be flattered). Think about practicalities: How you will get to the salon? Is there parking?; Are their appointment times likely to suit? Do they open at weekends or have a late night? Remember that the exterior of a salon can be deceptive, so have a look at the interior as well. Go in for a chat with one of the stylists – don't be shy as salons expect this to happen and should be happy to help.

Right *A visit to the salon should be a relaxing and enjoyable experience, so don't put up with service that's not perfect.*

What makes a good salon

The best hairdressers look after you from the moment you call to book, right through to when you leave. These days you should expect a good level of customer service as well as high standards in hairdressing itself. The salon should have regard for your comfort and safety, especially when using chemical processes such as colouring and perming solutions. Cleanliness should also be a priority – including the personal hygiene of the stylists.

What's a good haircut?

One you can maintain at home! It's really as simple as that. If you are as happy with your hair a week later as on the day you left the salon, then it's a good sign.

How to get good advice

Build up a rapport with your hairdresser. They are not mind-readers, so try to communicate well with them so that they can offer good advice. Show them pictures of styles you like on other people (you could take in this book and show them one of the looks in the gallery section), or photographs of looks you've enjoyed wearing in the past. Talk with them about your lifestyle and how much time you are willing to spend on your hair each day. It's no good asking for a high-maintenance look if you've not got time to devote to styling before you get going each day.

At every salon visit be interested in the products used on your hair – professional products are usually high-performance but cost more too, so make sure you understand how to get the best out of them. Be clear and honest about your haircare regimes and share any concerns you have about the condition of your hair and scalp.

How to get good service

It will help set things off on the right foot if you follow these simple guidelines:

- Turn up on time.
- Be fair.
- Give feedback.
- Take advice.
- If you have to cancel, give notice.
- Don't rush your stylist.

Above *Most salons pride themselves on being places where you can feel pampered, paying great attention to detail, including comfort.*

Above *It takes effort from both client and stylist to build up a good rapport and is certainly worth the effort.*

How to complain

It's important to speak up if you're not happy with a visit to the salon for whatever reason. The hairdresser or salon owner has a business to run, which relies not only on your custom but on satisfied customers' recommendations, so they should be grateful for the opportunity to put matters right and to be made aware of any problems.

To get the best results be clear about what it is that isn't right – is it the cut or colour, the service, treatment or price that bothers you? When you make the complaint at the salon, remember:

- Keep calm.
- Ask to see the salon manager.
- Set out what it is that you expected (in terms of hairstyle, service or price).
- Explain what it is that is different from what you expected.

If you realize that you're still not happy after you've left the salon then call the salon as soon as possible and ask to speak to the manager again. Explain once more what your expectations are and how they've not been met.

If your hair has been badly permed, don't accept any offer to have it re-permed, as this could exacerbate the problem. The remedy is to have a course of intensive conditioning treatments, which the salon may offer for free. Following this, you should wait until the hair is in optimum condition before you have another perm or colour treatment – this can unfortunately take a long time if you have long hair and you may want to consider having your hair shortened to remove some of the damaged hair and speed the recovery process.

If you feel you have suffered serious damage, for example an itchy, burning scalp, blisters, cuts, hair breakage or hair loss, then immediately seek advice from your family doctor or a trichologist. If they feel that you have cause for complaint and compensation, then ask them to prepare a report giving full details and an analysis of the problem. However, remember that hair grows, blisters heal, and memories fade, so act quickly and, if necessary, make sure you have some photographs taken at the time to reinforce your claim.

Cutting hair

Cutting hair properly is a skill that requires great expertise. To create a desired shape, it's important to know where weight and bulk needs to be removed to achieve a good line and balance, emphasize good points and detract from bad ones.

Hair growth varies over different parts of the head, which means that your cut can appear out of shape very quickly. As a general rule, a short, precision cut needs trimming every four weeks; a longer style every six to eight weeks. If you want to grow your hair long, it is essential to have it trimmed regularly – at least every three months – to prevent splitting and to keep the ends even. There are different ways to cut hair and even if you don't do it yourself, it's a good idea to have some understanding of techniques to help communicate more effectively with your hairdresser.

Classic cuts

Hairdressers learn the fundamental classic cuts, all of which can have variations to achieve different end results:

- **The one-length bob** is also known as a pageboy. It's a haircut where the hair falls to a one-length point that is the same all the way round the head (the perimeter) and usually sits above the shoulders. It's a useful way of making fine hair look thicker and more dense.

  Variations on a classic bob cut can then be used to individualize the look, such as making the front lengths longer than the back or vice versa. The hair is cut to form a smooth edge so that the lengths gradually rise or fall around the perimeter.

  The bob can be cut with or without a fringe (bangs) and with a central or side-parting. The hair can be blow-dried around a hairbrush to curl out or under, or combed to hang straight.
- **A long one-length cut** is where hair falls to a point below the shoulders. Again it can be personalized with or without a fringe and be blow-dried square-shaped or more rounded.
- **Layers** are where horizontal sections of hair are cut to the same length all round the head, so that in effect the haircut mirrors the head shape with top layers falling to a higher point than lower layers. It is useful for thinning out thick hair and removing bulk. You can have layers any length, from short to long,
- **Graduation** is a technique used to create top layers which are shorter than underneath layers. You can create a greater or lesser degree of graduation or create reverse graduation where underneath layers are shorter than top layers. It's an important technique for shaping styles.
- **A square-layered cut** is sometimes called box layers or graduated layers, and combines layering and graduation. It's called a square layer because if all the hair were blown back off the face it would form a square shape.
- **A round layered cut**, also called a French crop, is a basic layered shape where the hair is cut into rounded layers, creating a softer end shape.

Clockwise, from top left *Graduated cut with a fringe; long bob with a fringe; layered hair with a short fringe; long one-length hair.*

Above *Angling scissors will cut either blunt lines or chip into the ends of the hair, creating different finished effects.*

Top *A widow's peak can look very attractive if the hair is cut in a suitable style.*

Above *Cowlicks can be difficult to style or tame, so it is important that the hairdresser thinks carefully about how to cut the hair.*

Cutting techniques

Ways of cutting hair vary according to the effect you want to achieve, but there are several basic techniques that a hairdresser is likely to use:

- **Blunt cutting** is when the ends of the hair are cut straight across – often used for hair of one length or definite lines.
- **Point cutting** is where the scissors are pointed into the haircut to break up straight lines and add texture.
- **Slide cutting** is a way to thin thick hair and give a soft finish. This technique is often done when the hair is dry using open scissors to slice the hair.
- **Razor cutting** is literally using a razor rather than scissors, and creates softness, tapering, and internal movement so that the hair moves freely. It can also be used to shorten hair.
- **Thinning** is done either with thinning scissors or a razor; it removes bulk and weight without affecting the overall length of the hair.

Clever cuts

The art of hairdressing is in applying different techniques and cuts to make the most of a client's hair type and texture. These are some of the most common tricks of the trade:

- Fine, thin, flyaway hair can be given volume and movement by blunt cutting.
- Mid-length hair can benefit from being lightly layered to give extra volume.
- Short, thin hair can be blunt cut and the edges graduated to give movement.
- Some hairdressers razor-cut fine hair to give a thicker and more voluminous effect. It is best not to let fine hair grow too long. As soon as it reaches the shoulders it tends to look wispy.
- Thick and coarse hair can be controlled by reducing the weight to give more style. Avoid very short styles because the hair will stick out. Try a layered cut with movement.
- Layering also helps achieve height and eliminates weight. On shorter styles, the weight can be reduced with thinning scissors expertly used on the ends only.

Did you know?

Most salons offer the chance to return between appointments to request a fringe (bangs) be trimmed at no charge. It may be that you are expected to book, depending on how busy they are.

Styling problems

Sometimes hair grows in different directions, which may cause styling problems.

- **A cowlick** is found on the front hairline and occurs when the hair grows in a swirl, backwards and then forwards. Clever cutting can redistribute the weight and go some way to solving this problem.
- **A double crown** occurs when there are two pivots of natural hair at the top of the head, rather than the usual one. Styles with height at the crown are most suitable.
- **A widow's peak** is a descending point on the hairline, forming a V-shape, usually above the forehead. Taking hair in the reverse direction to the growth will give the impression of a natural wave.

Colouring hair

Beautiful hair is about condition and colour. You may be blessed with fantastic natural colour but still fancy a change, or maybe your own colouring needs a boost. Perhaps you like to change your hair tone as often as your clothes. The good news is, you can!

Technological advances in the past few years mean that hair colorants have never been better, both in terms of product efficiency and colour choice. You can now choose between temporary, semi-permanent, demi-permanent and permanent colour, Each offers a different lasting power depending on the base or natural colour, of your hair.

Different shades

Professional hair colours are made up of codes which follow an international numbering system. The first number refers to your natural hair colour, or base, and is counted from 0 (a natural blue/black) to 9 (extra light blonde). After a point, a second number indicates the tone of the hair. For instance, .0 is matt while .7 is violet. A third number indicates a secondary tone. So 6 will be Dark Blonde, while 6.4 indicates Dark Copper Blonde and 6.46 denotes Dark Copper Red Blonde.

It's not necessary to learn the numbering system but it can be useful to ask your hairdresser which numbers they have applied to create the colour you prefer.

Skin test

It's vital to do a skin test before using any colorant as some people are allergic to ingredients such as para-dyes, which appear in many products. An allergic reaction can range from mild itching to severe burning. Hairdressers should insist on doing a skin test 24 hours before applying colorants (beware any salons that don't) and most good products for home use now include a skin test, which you must perform. A small amount of product should be applied to a clean pulse point – behind the ear or in the crook of the elbow – and left for a minimum of 24 hours to check for any bad or allergic reaction.

Permanent colours

These colorants, or tints as they are often called, lighten or darken, and can very effectively cover white. While the colour is permanent, don't forget that roots will need retouching every 4–6 weeks to keep pace with new growth.

Permanent colorant works by putting colour pigment mixed with hydrogen peroxide into the cortex (the centre) of the hair shaft during the development time. The pigment adds melanin for darker shades of brown and black, and pheomelanin for red and yellow shades.

Left *The colour process can enhance the natural shine and condition of your hair, leaving it superbly healthy and attractive-looking.*

Above *There is a wide range of natural tones to choose from when you are looking for a new colour, as this colour swatch demonstrates.*

After the colorant is applied, the oxygen in the developer swells the pigments in the colorant until they comprise such large molecules that they can't escape from the cortex and so are locked in.

Another way of permanently changing hair colour is by lightening it using bleach with hydrogen peroxide (to activate the bleach) to de-colour the hair, creating a very light blonde. The peroxide enters the hair shaft by means of ammonia which lifts the cuticles. Once inside, the peroxide zaps the colour pigment in the hair, making it as light as you want. It's a harsh treatment so gentle aftercare is essential. Over-bleaching will destroy the hair so be very careful. For this reason, it's wise to get a professional to do a lightening process.

Semi-permanent colours

These are more gentle than permanent colorants as there is no ammonia or hydrogen peroxide to help the pigment penetrate the cortex. Instead, while it is absorbed into the cuticle layer and into the cortex, it stays only until it is washed out. The effect can only be used to add, enrich, or darken hair colour (semi-permanents cannot make hair any lighter). The colour fades gradually, washing away over several shampoos (12–20 depending on the manufacturer and the type of hair). They are ideal for those who want to experiment but don't want to commit to a permanent change; for blending in the first grey hairs; and for conditioning hair.

Demi-permanent colours

Halfway between a permanent and a semi-permanent, demi-permanent colorant includes a small amount of hydrogen peroxide but no ammonia. It won't change the existing pigment but it will deposit more colour in the hair shaft, enhancing natural colour and covering grey. There isn't such obvious regrowth as with permanent treatments, since colour is added rather then altered, and it's kinder than permanent colour. However, it will still only last up to 20 washes.

Temporary colours

These are mild colorants that last about 1–5 washes, depending on the porosity of the hair. They work by coating the outside, or cuticle layer, of the hair but do not penetrate the cortex as there is no hydrogen peroxide in them. However, if the hair is damaged and the cuticle open, parts of the hair can trap colour molecules. In this case, hair must be conditioned and the cuticle smoothed before applying. Temporary colours are good for a quick change or for counteracting discoloration. They come in mousse, hairspray, setting lotion, gel, glitter dust or cream formulations.

Did you know?

- *Colouring swells the hair shaft, making fine hair appear thicker.*
- *Because colour changes the porosity of the hair it can help combat greasiness.*
- *Rich tones reflect more light and give hair a thicker appearance.*
- *Highlights give fine hair extra texture and break up the heaviness of very thick hair.*

Below *Hair colour is applied via different techniques. Foils are popular and are a great way of putting fine highlights through the hair.*

Below *Colorants can be mixed to create virtually any shade, tone and intensity you desire. Professional colourists are true artists.*

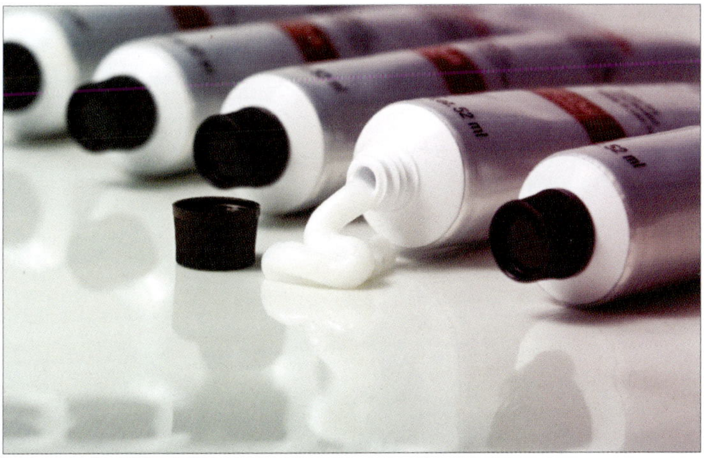

Choosing a colour

Thinking of taking the plunge for the first time and having your hair coloured? Or perhaps you're looking for a fresh new look? But what to choose? Ask friends and professionals for advice – consultations in salons are often free even if you go on to do it yourself at home.

Colouring basics

Before you have your hair coloured, there are several things you should consider:

- Think about skin tone. If you're after a natural look then you don't want something that clashes with your skin.
- When choosing a colour, a basic rule is to keep to one or two shades at each side of your original tone.
- Only have a colour change if your hair is in good condition: dry, porous hair absorbs colour too rapidly, leading to a patchy result.
- A few highlights or lowlights put through your natural colour is a good introduction to colour without heavy commitment.
- Temporary colour is a great way of testing out what you like best.
- Tone on tone is a technique to blend white hair with natural hair colour, or to blend and create evenness. It lasts 2–4 weeks and adds depth, sheen and life to hair.
- Collect pictures of hair colours you like and compare them with the hair tufts on colourists' charts.

Highlights and lowlights

These terms apply to fine to medium strands of lighter or darker colour woven through the hair. Sometimes they are applied as fine slices, especially on thicker or more curly hair. The effect can be amazing, particularly if done by a professional. Lighter pieces around the face can really open up your features and accentuate dark eyes. Adding darker pieces around the face will accentuate light eyes.

Natural dyes

Made from herbs and plants, natural dyes can provide a semi-permanent colour for highlights or lowlights, but they can't change your appearance dramatically or cover grey completely, as they generally don't penetrate the cortex.

The vibrancy and durability of these shades depends on the condition of the hair and the depth of shade you are trying to achieve. Equally the quality of the raw ingredients comes into play, combined with the porosity and natural colour of your hair.

Although henna is the most widely used natural dye, others can be extracted from a wide variety of plants, including marigold petals, cloves, rhubarb stalks and even tea leaves. Henna enhances natural highlights, making colour appear richer. It is available today as a powder, which is mixed with water to form a paste. The colour fades gradually, but frequent applications will give a stronger, longer-lasting effect. On brunette or black hair henna produces a lovely reddish glow, while lighter hair becomes a beautiful titian. Please note, however, that henna will not lighten, and it is not suitable for use on blonde hair. On hair that is more than 20 per cent grey, white, tinted, bleached or highlighted, the resultant colour will be orange!

Colouring at home

Many people choose to colour their hair at home because it is cheaper and more convenient. Today, home colorants are much improved but they are still arguably harsher on the hair and give different results from those from a salon dye. A good colouring job is also very much about where the colour is placed, which is why, if you are choosing an intricate look such as highlights, it really is best to go to a salon. If you are careful, however, an all-over tint can work well at home.

In addition to reading the instructions and following them accurately, there are some basic rules that you should follow:

- Always do a skin test first and wait 24 hours before proceeding. If you have an allergic reaction it can be painful, so don't take risks.

Left *Think about the condition of the hair before applying colour so you get the best result.*

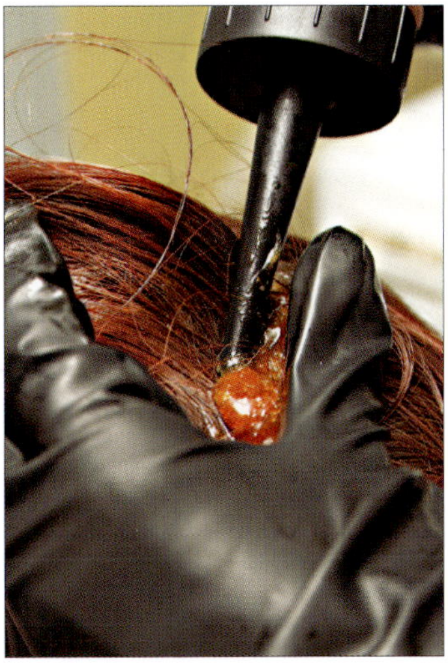

- Never mix products from different packs, as this could cause a bad reaction.
- Keep to the times given in the instructions to avoid over-processing.
- Try semi-permanent colouring first, until you are more experienced.
- Choose colour carefully and opt for a lighter shade than you want, as many home-colour products turn out darker than indicated.
- Get someone to check you've applied the product evenly.
- Apply colour to reasonably clean but not squeaky clean hair – the natural levels of sebum will help protect your scalp.
- Use a cream or petroleum jelly around your hairline to protect your skin from absorbing colour.

White hair

If you just want to cover a few white hairs, use a temporary colour, which lasts 1–5 washes, or semi-permanent colour, which will last for 6–12 washes. Choose a tone that is similar to your natural colour. If the hair is brown, applying a warm brown colour will pick out the white areas and give lighter chestnut highlights. Alternatively, henna will give a glossy finish and produce stunning red highlights. For salt-and-pepper hair (hair with a mixed amount of white with the natural colour), try a longer-lasting, tone-on-tone colour. These last for 20 washes and also add shine.

When hair is completely white, it can be covered with a permanent tint. With this type of colorant it is necessary to update the colour every four to six weeks, a fact that should be taken into consideration before choosing this option. Those who prefer to stay with their natural shade of white can improve on the colour by using temporary colorants such as toning shampoos, conditioners and styling products, which will remove any brassiness and add beautiful silvery tones.

Care for coloured hair

Chlorinated and salt water, perspiration, and the weather all conspire to fade coloured hair, particularly red hair. However, special haircare products are available that will help counteract fading, such as those containing ultraviolet filters that protect coloured hair from the effects of the sun. Other protective measures include rinsing the hair after swimming and using a shampoo designed for coloured hair, or those that put up a barrier between the hair and chlorinated water, followed by a separate conditioner. Gently blot the hair after shampooing – never rub it vigorously as this ruffles the cuticle and can result in colour 'escaping'. Finally, use an intensive conditioning treatment at least once a month.

Above left *Colorants are fantastic at achieving all levels of cover, including 100 per cent white. Consult your salon for advice or look for products specifically designed to do this.*

Above *Your skin will absorb colour so wear gloves for all colour work.*

Colour correction

If you have been colouring your hair for some time and want to go back to your natural colour and tone, consult a professional hairdresser.

Right *For home colouring, equipping yourself with a proper colour mixing bowl and brush will make the whole job a lot easier.*

Chemical treatments

Women have always craved the ability to make their straight hair more curly or to smooth away natural waves and curl. It's possible to style hair between washes, but this requires effort so more permanent treatments are great time-savers.

Although the way perms (for waving or curling hair) and relaxants (for straightening hair) work hasn't changed significantly over the years, they are being constantly refined and improved so they are kinder to hair. Essentially they operate by chemically altering the inner structure of the hair and re-fixing it in a different shape.

Some new products are able to scan the hair to detect variations in porosity, while others will rectify damage or loosen a perm that has been set too tight. Semi-permanent waves are also now available, and these add volume without having to commit to permanent tight curl. They can be applied all over or at the root area in particular to add lift to flat hair.

Preparation for chemical treatments

Hair should be washed prior to perming or relaxing as this causes the scales on the cuticles to rise gently, allowing the perm/relaxant lotion to enter the hair shaft more quickly. However, the scalp should not be rubbed too vigorously as this will increase sensitivity to the chemical solutions.

How do chemical treatments work?

First, either an acid-balanced or alkaline wave lotion is applied to the hair. This alters the keratin and breaks down the sulphur bonds that link the fibre-like cells in the inner layers of each hair. When these have become loose, they can be formed into a new shape, either straight or curled depending on whether the hair is stretched over a curler or a perm rod. The development time can vary according to the condition and texture of the hair.

Left *Ever-advancing technology means both perming and straightening techniques are improving, becoming kinder to the hair.*

When the development is complete, the changed links in the hair are re-formed into their new shape by the application of a second chemical known as the neutralizer. This contains an oxidizing agent that is effectively responsible for closing up the broken links and producing the wave, curl or straighter section – permanently.

Home versus salon

Perming and relaxing are such delicate operations that many women prefer to leave it in the hands of experienced, professional hairdressers. Although perming at home is considerably cheaper, the advantages of having hair processed in a salon are:

- The hair is first carefully analyzed to see whether it is in a fit condition to take the chemical process. Hair that is coloured, out-of-condition, or over-processed may not be suitable.
- There is a greater choice in the type of result available at a salon – different strengths of lotion and winding techniques give a range of curls that are not easily achieved at home.

Don't do it if...

- Your hair is very dry or damaged.
- You have bleached or highlighted your hair: it may be too fragile.
- The traces of an old perm still remain.
- You suffer from a scalp disorder such as eczema or have broken, irritated skin.

Different types of perm

Bear in mind the choices include:

- **Acid perms** produce highly conditioned, flexible curls with a soft curl pattern. The acid enters the hair slowly, so heat is used to speed up the process. They are gentler than alkaline perms, making them suited to hair that is fine, sensitive, fragile, damaged or tinted.

Above left *You can create different results by winding hair on to rollers or bendy rods, placed either horizontally or vertically in the hair.*

Above *You can achieve a wide range of results using modern perming techniques, including tight curls.*

- **Alkaline perms** are able to offer strong curl patterns, with a fast processing time at room temperature – no heat is required. They give striking, firm curl results on normal and resistant hair. They should not be used on more delicate or damaged hair.
- **Exothermic perms** give bouncy, resilient curls and are suitable for most hair types. 'Exothermic' refers to the gentle heat that is produced by the chemical reaction that occurs when the lotion is mixed. The heat allows the chemicals to penetrate the hair cuticle, conditioning and strengthening the hair from inside as the lotion moulds the hair into its new shape.

Above *More traditional rigid curlers come in a range of sizes – often colour coded for ease of use. They are great for home or salon use.*
Left *Bendable rods are comfortable and great for winding the hair for a more natural looking result. Try wrapping a disposable paper around the mid-section of the rod in order to prevent lotion penetrating the covering of the rod and damaging its surface.*

Perming techniques

Any of the types of perm listed on the preceding page can be used with different techniques to produce a number of results:

- **Body perms** are very soft, loose perms created by using large curlers, or sometimes rollers, to wind the hair. The result is added volume with a hint of wave and movement, rather than curls.
- **Root perms** add lift and volume to the root area only. They give height and fullness, and are therefore ideal for short hair that tends to go flat.
- **Pin curl perms** give soft, natural waves and curls, which are achieved by perming small sections of hair that have been pinned into pre-formed curls.
- **Stack perms** give curl and volume to one-length haircuts and are created using lots of different-sized curlers to wind the hair. The hair on top of the head is left unpermed while the middle and ends are given curl and movement.
- **Spiral perms** create romantic spiral curls, an effect that is produced by winding the hair around special, long curlers. The mass of curls usually makes longer hair look much thicker.
- **Spot perms** give support only on the area to which they are applied. For example, if the hair needs lift, the perm is applied just on the crown, creating height and volume in that area. They can also be used on the fringe (bangs) or side areas around the face.
- **Weave perms** involve perming certain sections of hair and leaving the rest straight to give a mixture of texture and natural-looking body and bounce, particularly on areas around the face such as the fringe.

Home rules

If you do use a perm at home, it is essential that you read and follow the instructions supplied with the product.

- Remember to do a test curl to check whether your hair is suitable, and check to make certain you have enough curlers.
- You will probably want to enlist the help of a friend, as it's virtually impossible to curl the back sections of your own hair properly, so you'll need a helping hand.
- Timing is crucial – don't be tempted to remove the lotion before the time given or leave it on longer than directed.

Curl result

As with any curl (other than natural curls), the size and type depends on a number of factors:

- The size of the curler determines the size of the curl. Generally, the smaller the diameter, the smaller (and tighter) the curl, whereas medium to large diameter curlers tend to give a much looser effect.
- The strength of lotion used can make a difference, as can the texture and type of hair. Hair in good condition takes a perm better than hair in poor condition, and fine hair curls more easily than coarse hair.
- After a perm it takes 48 hours for the keratin in the hair to harden naturally. During this time the hair is vulnerable and must be treated with great care.

Resist shampooing, brushing, vigorous combing, blow-drying or setting, any of which may cause it to drop.

▪ Once hair has been permed it remains shaped the way it has been formed, although new growth will be straight. As time goes by, the curl can soften and loosen, and if the hair is long, its weight may make the curl and the wave appear much looser.

Disappointed?

If the results of a perm are not what you expected, it could be that some of the following apply:

▪ **Uneven curl** Lotion was misapplied and hasn't been able to penetrate evenly. You need a salon or hairdressing professional to assess whether another perm can be applied safely.

▪ **Curls too tight or frizzy** Product was left on too long, or maybe an incorrect choice of curlers or rod size was used. Relax the hair by blow-drying and heavy conditioning or contact a salon to see if they can give you a curl relaxer.

▪ **Hair falling out in clumps** Rollers were wound too tight or the hair was combed badly in a relaxer phase. See a hairdresser – this needs professional help and you can't fix it yourself.

▪ **Hair meltdown** If hair loses all its elasticity as a result of over-processing it can feel very strange indeed. Avoid over-moisturizing and choose conditioners that add strength.

Below *Perming the hair need not mean any loss of condition or manageability provided the right processes were followed.*

Below *Wait 48 hours before washing newly treated hair and ensure you use specially formulated shampoos and conditioners.*

Post-treatment tips

Having done the deed, you now need to treat your hair carefully and follow a few simple rules:

▪ Don't wash newly-processed hair for 48 hours afterwards as any stress can cause the effect to change.

▪ Use specialist shampoos and conditioners formulated for chemically-treated hair. They help retain the correct moisture balance and prolong the new shape. Your hairdresser will be able to advise which you should use.

▪ Always use a wide-toothed comb and work from the ends upwards. Never brush the hair.

▪ Blot wet hair dry before styling, to prevent it stretching.

▪ Avoid using too much heat on fragile hair. If possible, wash, condition, then leave hair to dry naturally.

▪ If your perm has lost its bounce, mist it with water or try a curl reviver. These are designed to put instant volume and bounce into permed hair. They are also ideal for eliminating frizziness on naturally curly hair.

▪ Expect your perm or relaxed hair to last three to six months, depending on the technique and lotion used.

▪ Don't use metal combs or hairgrips (bobby pins) on newly relaxed hair.

Asian and Afro hair

Styling Afro or Asian hair can often be challenging. The good news is that as product formulations and the expertise of hairdressers improves, there is more technical knowledge of how to create fantastic hairstyles, whatever your hair type.

Asian hair

Usually very dark, straight and naturally shiny, Asian can be so heavy and straight that it lacks body and texture, unable to support styles requiring volume. Often to add guts, you need to turn to chemical texturizing methods including perming and body waves, although clever stylists can layer the hair to create more movement and lift. Perming just the first length of hair nearest the scalp can provide great root lift without giving unwanted curl. Adding a little colour or lightening some sections of the hair can also achieve depth and texture.

Afro hair

Often more dry, brittle and fine than other ethnic types, Afro hair needs extra hydration and care to promote healthy growth. It will most often be curly, although the degree of wave varies enormously. The reason for it being fragile is because the sebaceous glands produce insufficient sebum to moisturize the hair. In addition, because the hair is tightly curled, the sebum is unable to travel downwards to condition it naturally. If the curl forms kinks, this makes the hair thinner, and therefore weaker, at each bend.

It's vital to keep this type of hair oiled – how often will depend on the texture and your individual needs – perhaps every day, perhaps two or three times a week. Don't be tempted to reduce washing as the scalp needs regular cleansing. Do use a good moisturizing conditioner each time you shampoo. Hair that is chemically treated (permed, relaxed or coloured) in particular will need protein and moisture. Use a wide-tooth comb to avoid breaking fragile hair. Some people swear by the mantra 'condition, wash, then condition again'. Remember to rinse Afro hair very thoroughly; where detergents are not well rinsed away, you may suffer a contact reaction, the side effects of which include irritation, inflammation and dandruff.

Chemical treatments

While Asian hair can benefit from being permed to add body and movement, Afro hair can be relaxed or straightened, which is in fact perming in reverse. This process, also known as a chemical relaxing, involves chemicals being combed or worked through the hair to change the structure of the hair and to straighten it. The result is permanent, only disappearing as the hair grows.

As with all chemical treatments, relaxing, perming and colouring can be potentially harmful to the hair, removing natural moisture and leaving hair in a weakened state. For this reason it is advisable to get skilled professional help and advice.

- **Chemical relaxers** come in different strengths to suit different hair textures and styles. They are particularly effective on longer styles as the weight of the hair helps to maintain the straightened look. If you want to straighten your hair at home it is important to get advice first, and make sure you use high-quality, branded products and follow the instructions precisely to get the best results.

Far left *Asian hair is often very dark in colour but can be lightened or coloured by lifting out the natural colour then applying new colorant.*

Left *Afro hair can usually be straightened very successfully using a process often referred to as 'relaxing' the hair.*

▪ **Advanced perms** involve softening the hair by weaving it on to rollers and then neutralizing it so that the curls are permanently set into their new shape. This should be done at a salon.

To prevent frizziness and maintain the definition of curls, special lotions called curl activators and moisturizing sprays can be used to revive and preserve the formation of curls.

▪ **Colouring** Afro hair can be tricky to handle, because it is naturally dry and porous, so it is worth seeking professional advice when considering colouring it. If the hair has been straightened, relaxed or permed, it may be too weak to colour successfully. Techniques such as highlighting, low-lighting, or tipping the ends are best for this type of hair.

Asian hair can usually be coloured successfully but will need the dark base colour removing (or you risk orange results). This is called lifting. Once the natural colour has been lifted then it's possible to achieve the same colour results as on Caucasian hair.

Non-chemical treatments

Very curly hair can also be tamed by demi-perming. This enables tight curls to be replaced by larger, looser ones. Demi-perms are good for short hair, giving a more controlled, manageable shape, while on long hair they produce a softer, bouncier look. Made with pineapple enzyme, the treatment is good for children and those who are sensitive to chemical relaxers.

Dreadlocks, braids and weaves

▪ **Dreadlocks** are when sections of hair are twisted together starting a short way down the hair from the scalp. The name refers to the way the hair is locked together and can't be untwisted. Oil, such as almond oil, or wax, such as beeswax, should be applied to the hair before twisting and then the hair can be washed in mild shampoo. The only way to loosen them is to have them cut out.

▪ **Braids** (off-the-scalp plaits) and cornrows (on-the-scalp plaits) are a popular way to style the hair and keep it close to the head. They can be removed when you wish, although be careful not to leave them in too long or the hair will mesh together and be hard to loosen.

▪ **Weaves** are a type of hair extension technique that uses strands of hair attached to existing hair with specially formulated hair adhesives. This is a good method for those who want long lasting wear, from 3 to 6 months.

Special problems

Traction hair loss is caused by braiding or weaving hair too tightly. If the hair is pulled too forcibly too often, it will disrupt the hair follicles, cause scar tissue to form and ultimately result in hair loss. To help prevent this, avoid braiding or pulling the hair into tight braids. Similar problems can also result from misusing perming and relaxing chemicals. If you do experience problems it is important to consult your salon.

Above *Asian hair is usually very thick, straight and glossy, and fantastic shine can often be achieved simply by combing it through.*

Did you know?

Hair needs to be strong and healthy to take any type of chemical treatment. To check hair strength and natural elasticity, pluck out a hair and hold it firmly between the fingers of both hands, then pull gently. If the hair breaks with hardly any stretching, it is weak and in poor condition, in which case all chemical treatments should be avoided.

Far right *Long, fine braids that hang away from the scalp can be worn down or up, in much the same way as non-braided hair.*

Right *Cornrow braids lie on the scalp and are different from plaits or braids, which hang away from the scalp.*

Choosing a style

Choosing a new hairstyle can be an exciting prospect. Altering the cut, colour or texture of your hair is an instant way to transform your appearance and can be such a boost to your confidence. But the choice of what to go for can be overwhelming. We've gathered ideas on short, mid-length, long and curly looks to both demonstrate the variety of looks out there and also to inspire you in your quest for a new look and a new you. Browse these galleries of headshots – whether bold and daring or more subtle and understated, there are so many ways to wear your hair. Let's go!

Shorter hair

Short hair can be the most flattering and stylish of cuts and there are many different ways to wear the look.

1 Short, textured layers give this style a fashionable finish, with just the merest suggestion of a fringe (bangs). Since it is so short, very little finishing product is required to achieve the look; it's all in the cut.

2 This striking coppery crop can be created by blow-drying hair smooth using a paddle brush, then spritzing it all over with shine spray to show off superb colour to the max.

3 Here, a deep, sweeping fringe adds individuality and drama to what is essentially a classic, round-cut short crop. A smooth, glossy finish and rich, uniform colour completes the effect.

4 Blonde shades can be stunning on short styles, but you should always ask your hairdresser for advice on what tones will suit your complexion best.

5 Bring out the texture of a short cut by applying a small amount of a soft, matte molding paste. Simply piece the paste through the mid-lengths and ends of your hair.

6 An angular perimeter gives a retro feel to this sharp, short cut. Blow-dry the hair super-smooth and add plenty of shine spray for a sleek, glossy finish.

7 This cute elfin cut is a timeless classic that is best suited to striking face shapes and clear complexions. Slightly longer layers on top can be worn smooth or textured, depending on the effect you want to achieve.

8 Add definition and contrast with low-lights of golden honey tones, which add depth and shape to a very short cut. Brushing the hair forward emphasizes great bone structure.

1

2

3

4

5

6

7

8

9

10

11

12

9 A short crop cut close in around the ears still retains the feel of plenty of movement due to texture at the crown, which can help to balance a longer face shape. Shaping or molding pastes add definition and keep the fringe (bangs) swept to one side.

10 A neat, angular jaw-length cut draws attention to a great mouth, while the strong, deep fringe helps focus attention on fantastic eyes. Emphasize great condition of the hair using a slick of finishing crème or shine spray for a glossy result.

11 Longer front sections pushed to one side are both cute and edgy. The trick here is to piece through a styling crème or light wax to hold the definition.

12 Brushing hair forward on a short cut is very stylish and shows off a jagged perimeter, which is very individual. It also frames the face and reveals a good head shape. Strong-hold finishing sprays are the key to keeping the style in place.

13 Blow-drying hair and wrapping sections round a barrel brush enhances volume and shows off the health and vitality of well-groomed hair.

14 When adding colour to a shorter cut, blending a selection of shades gives a gorgeous, natural look and enhances the texture.

15 After blow-drying cropped hair to pull it forward, piece styling wax through the front section to add definition and shine.

16 Honey blonde highlights shot through brunette tones add warmth and depth to a very simple cut. A strong perimeter shape is fantastic and accentuates full lips and strong cheek bones beautifully.

17 White-blonde hair colour can be particularly eye-catching if you have the complexion to carry it off. A deep fringe and shaped perimeter update a classic bob and create a stiking, modern look.

18 A short cut with no fringe is a versatile look – change the parting to suit your mood and using smoothing and styling products for shine and to hold in place.

13

14

15

16

17

18

19 A shattered perimeter is dramatic and stylish on a one-length cut, especially if colour is applied to bring out the sense of shape.

20 On a layered, short cut, ring the changes by tonging sections at the crown then raking through with your fingers to create texture and height to contrast with a smooth front section.

21 Leaving a section of hair to fall forward on a short round cut is eye-catching, and adds some softness and individuality on what could be a severe style.

22 When trying to grow out a short crop, go with a transition cut with graduated layers, which are short yet stylish.

23 Smooth the fringe (bangs) area on a choppy cut for contrast. Tease or back-brush the remaining areas to bring out the texture, then spray to hold.

19

20

21

22

23

24

25

26

27

28

29

24 A smooth, short cut shows off superb condition on healthy hair. Here, the fringe and side areas are connected for a very round look, which looks best on fine face shapes with delicate features.

25 Longer front sections and a higher back creates a very stylish, dramatic look. You will need confidence to pull it off, but it's a real show-stopper when you do. Keep it super-sleek for maximum effect.

26 For a more casual, tousled look on a layered short cut, first blast dry hair for texture, then tip your head forward and run your fingers through the hair for a looser, freer movement.

27 A chic, sleek bob with sharply defined perimeter is a look of timeless elegance. Blow-drying hair absolutely smooth and sleek is the ultimate way to show off a great head shape.

28 When blow-drying a joined-up bob, try pulling layers forward to show off a deep fringe area, then use styling products to define the texture and hold hair in place.

29 A very blunt fringe, longer side sections and a high, graduated back are reminiscent of the 1920s – a look that works very well with strong features. Blow-drying and tousling the back for texture brings the look bang up to date.

30 For a more glamorous and groomed finish on a short cut, push the short side sections back, then tong the crown to accentuate height.

31 On a short cut that retains some longer internal layers, blow-dry hair at the back to flick out the ends while keeping the sides smooth. It creates a more intriguing look than a traditional finish.

32 Hair with a curl or strong wave can look fantastic when cut with plenty of layering to add shape. Leave hair to dry naturally to show off the movement. Apply serum to the ends of the hair to prevent frizziness.

33 Blast-dry short hair for maximum movement and volume, then tease sections for lift. Finally smooth a single front piece to add contrast.

30

31

32

33

34

35

36

37

38

34 Wear a classic bob cut in a looser way by drying the hair smooth, then spritzing all over with flexible spray and messing up the layers using your fingers.

35 For a funky look on a very short crop, simply apply plenty of gel with a hold factor through the top layers. It adds extra vitality and strength.

36 Long layers on a bob cut are a superb way to show off a vibrant colour and great head shape. The lightest of blondes reflects fantastic shine.

37 A smooth classic bob is given an edge with a fringe worn higher than usual, showing off fantastic eyebrows.

38 For a very dramatic, upswept look, first blow-dry hair round a hairbrush to add lift at the roots, then draw hair back up to the crown and fix with plenty of strong-hold spray to accentuate the upward movement.

39 Emulate the feel of a retro quiff by backcombing longer sections at the roots and using gel and spray to hold in place.

40 For a look with real impact, keep one section of hair at the front extra long on a short crop. Crimp or tease this longer hair so that it contrasts with the smoothness of the remaining hair.

39

40

Mid-length hair

The beauty of hair that falls below the chin and sits around the shoulders is that it can be styled differently from one day to the next, and cut to suit different face shapes.

1 Shattered layers cut through a square mid-length shape with a fringe (bangs) reduce internal weight and add texture as well as showing off a strong colour.

2 Applying irons brings out the cut of a mid-length style, emphasizing the smooth connection from the fringe area to the sides. A slick of smoothing crème or spritz of shine spray is perfect to finish.

3 For interest and individuality, longer front sections are chopped into and blow-dried to flick out, creating a flattering softness around the face.

4 A choice of fiery and vibrant red tones is stunning and helps lifts a very straight-forward one-length cut to be extremely eye-catching. Be careful to use colour-saving care products to keep your new look turning heads as long as possible!

5 Fabulous auburn tones in a strongly layered cut are particularly eye-catching, showing off hair that is in great condition.

6 For a dramatic look, the perimeter of this style is cut shorter at the back than the front. A razor-sharp, exaggerated fringe adds to the style's dynamic feel.

7 Setting a parting very low makes a longer front section fall across the eye for a playful effect, while remaining hair is swept back to leave the neckline clean.

8 Pale golden blondes and defined layers put through a mid-length cut can look ethereal, especially on pale skin tones.

1

2

3

4

5

6

7

8

9

10

11

12

9 Shoulder-length hair with a fringe (bangs) can be blow-dried super-smooth, then tucked under and gripped in place at the hairline to suggest a super-wide, sleek bob.

10 On thick hair, a mid-length bob with only the suggestion of a fringe can look really gentle and feminine. Blow-dry to create volume and softness and use hairspray to hold the shape.

11 Long layers and an exaggerated cheek-length fringe section pulled over the face makes fine hair look more full and makes it easier to tame. Smoothing products help to calm flyaways.

12 Mid-length hair set on large rollers is then allowed to tumble how it pleases to conjure up a mood of effortless elegance.You can pin up longer sections to create volume and shape.

13 A volumizing mousse applied to the roots and mid-lengths before blow-drying mid-length hair helps achieve width and strength through extra root lift. Curling sections around a large-barrel hairbrush adds movement.

14 For a didn't-try-too-hard glamorous look, try tonging hair through the mid-lengths and ends, then turning under the perimeter of shoulder-length hair and pinning in place. Don't make it too clean and tease out loose ends for a free, almost candy-floss prettiness.

15 For a high-impact party look, run straightening irons over layered mid-length hair to show off the cut and wear with a low-parting so hair falls over one eye.

16 A strong, deep fringe contrasts with the shattered perimeter on a mid-length bob shape. Fine highlights are shown off through the smoother top front section.

17 A head of sleek hair is a chic look. To achieve perfection, hair is blow-dried super smooth then straightening irons applied before hair is spritzed all over with shine spray.

18 Long wispy layers add innocence and femininity to mid-length styles. This look works particularly well on fine hair.

19 For a fun, avant-garde look, hairpieces can be colour-matched with natural hair and blended to give volume and shape.

20 Set shoulder-length hair on rollers to add guts and volume, then sweep up to the crown to form a roll and grip in place.

21 Shoulder-length hair offers scope for creating strong looks. Here, the front section is backcombed and rolled to form a quiff, and the back section back-brushed for volume.

22 A close-cut mid-length bob shows off superb shine, colour and condition. Longer front sections add an individual dynamic and keep the look fresh.

23 Shattered edges on the perimeter of a bob, with graduated sides chopped into, is a modern take on a screen siren style.

24 A neat mid-length bob shape shows off great facial features and can soften a heavy or square jawline. It's perfect for showcasing statement colour, too.

25 A hidden panel of colour on long layers adds an individual touch and provides versatility on a classic cut.

19

20

21

22

23

24

25

26 To give the illusion of an elfin crop on mid-length hair, simply smooth it into a neat, low ponytail or bun. Calm flyaways with hairspray for a super-sleek finish.

27 Pinning up sections of wavy mid-length hair, rather than tying it back with a hairband (headband), creates a soft, pretty finish and showcases flawless skin. Position a mirror so you can see the back of your head to help you achieve this style.

28 A simple, neat ballerina bun can look stunning. Wear it for almost any occasion, from school or work to evening events. It is a look that opens up a petite face and shows off great eyebrows.

29 A softer take on the classic bun can be created by leaving tendrils of hair loose at the front, which helps frame the face and provides softness.

30 For a deliberately messed-up back-do, be casual as you draw hair off the face – it's a less severe look.

31 Use your fingers to rake through hair and sweep it into a chignon (twist the loose ends and pin at the back of the head). Don't worry about tendrils falling free – it's part of the charm.

32 Strong, thick mid-length hair can be cut into a layered style that is easy to look after and looks fabulous. Use a round brush to shape the hair when blow-drying and apply conditioning spray and shine spray to calm any frizz.

33 For hair with natural curl or movement, accentuate the texture by first applying curl-defining crème, then diffuse-drying the hair for a soft finish. Don't be tempted to brush it or you will create volume rather than shape.

34 A one-length bob can be encouraged to curl sweetly by tonging through the mid-lengths and ends then blending the curl, rather than leaving as ringlets, for a grown-up finish.

35 Afro hair that is relaxed can still be worn in waves, rather than having to stick to the super-straight finish. Ask your salon for advice on the best products for your hair type.

32

33

34

35

36

37

38

36 Volumizing mousse and curl-defining crème add width and texture to this style. Avoid a fringe (bangs) for a more sophisticated vibe.

37 Dark, sleek hair shines gorgeously, and when cut into layers and encouraged to wave or curl is both sultry and glamorous. Simply spritz with shine spray to calm flyaways and add gloss.

38 With clever placement, using several colour tones through the hair will pick out shine lines and make hair appear more lustrous and healthy.

39 A dramatically layered cut adds lots of texture to a style – especially on fine hair – and helps draw attention to features such as beautiful eyes and cheekbones.

40 A very long fringe can be swept across one eye and smoothed with shine cream for a great peek-a-boo effect.

39

40

Longer hair

Wearing hair to fall below the shoulders is the perfect way to show off great condition and colour. From gorgeous curl to amazing shine, the choice of looks is endless.

1 A deep fringe (bangs) adds a great individual touch to one-length longer hair. Keep it trimmed ultra-straight so it sits just above the eyes and use smoothing crème or serum to keep it looking glossy.

2 Bringing out superb depth and shine, gorgeous auburn tones are expertly applied to very long hair. With hair this long, it is essential that you maintain great condition.

3 Asian hair is usually very straight, thick and glossy, so it is perfect for a longer style. Here, a blunt, deep fringe frames the face and provides contrast with the very long lengths.

4 Darker shades on smoother hair will give maximum opportunity to create shine as light reflects better and brings out the health of the hair. When blow-drying, apply volumizing products to the roots to encourage lift in this area.

5 Simple curls tonged through the lower sections of straight hair ring the changes and add body and interest. Don't be tempted to break up the curl, leave it to fall naturally. Here, top back sections are pinned to create height.

6 A very smooth, straight fringe is contrasted with more tousled longer lengths for a groomed look that is stunning yet understated.

7 Layers cut into very long lengths help to avoid a block feel on this style, and add some sense of movement and texture. Here, contrasting extensions are used to exaggerate the length. Use shine spray to calm flyaways.

1

2

3

4

5

6

7

8

9

10

11

8 When blow-drying longer hair, the very ends of the hair can be wrapped around a large-barrel hairbrush to encourage them to kick out and show off front layers.

9 For a rich, luminous depth of colour, blend blonde tones from pale to darker golds and style hair in sultry waves.

10 Playing with different tones of chocolate and mahogany creates a glorious brunette finish that brings out the depth and condition of long hair. Naturally wavy hair can look good with long sections in the front, which are encouraged to sweep back off the face, adding softness to the look.

11 Long, blonde hair is a fresh and youthful look. Creating gentle curls through the front section makes a great face-framer and ups the glamour factor on long, one-length hair.

12 A zig-zag parting allows hair to sweep forward without dragging hair into two parts. It can disguise regrowth on highlights, too.

13 Blonde hair with golden tones put through can look fabulous when simply groomed smooth and sleek to show off great shine. A dab of serum keeps everything in place and looking neat.

14 Volume and texture are achieved on longer, fine hair by crimping small sections of hair, then teasing out underneath layers to create as much volume a possible.

15 Ironing the mid-lengths and ends of very long hair will emphasize the look. It's extremely important to take good care of long hair, especially on the older, more tired ends, which require regular trimming. Deep-conditioning treatments are best.

16 Body is added to thin or fine hair by having layers cut through and then applying product before blast-drying. Colour helps plump out fine hair, too.

17 On long one-length hair where there is not a style as such, have fun with high- and lowlights and add curl and wave to keep the look intriguing and beautiful.

12

13

14

15

16

17

18 For exaggerated volume and height and to open up the face, backcomb hair at the roots, then draw hair to the back of the head, smoothing top sections as you go. Apply a strong-hold spray to finish.

19 Loose blonde hair with long layers creates a casual yet pretty look. Ensure hair is tangle-free and add hairspray to the roots to add guts and volume.

20 Soft layering through the hair allows it to spring up and reveals the natural texture and colour. This is a classic look that remains sweet and feminine.

21 A fiery red colour adds a touch of magic to longer, straighter hair. With some long layers through the sides, try shaping the style so it doesn't have a parting, to allow hair to fall forward softly.

22 Avoid wearing a fringe (bangs) on a small face with a low forehead. Instead, let it fall naturally, as this will open up and balance the face.

23 Blow-dry hair wrapped around a large-barrelled brush to create soft waves in the hair, rather than curls.

24 Long hair can be tonged through the mid-lengths and curled at the ends with large-barrelled irons to create wave, volume and movement.

25 Lightly backbrush very long hair at the roots to add volume and lift, without looking like you have tried too hard.

18

19

20

21

26

27

28

29

26 Generous ringlets on extra-long hair is an archetypal romantic look. It's a theatrical alternative to a formal up-do on special occasions.

27 Thick, long hair with shorter front layers looks luxurious and full of body. It's very versatile too.

28 If you're lucky to have thick, healthy hair then enjoy the freedom of wearing it loose and not set. Simply apply serum to the ends for extra shine.

29 There's something demure about a central parting and it can be the perfect way to frame a neat face and open up the eyes.

30 On very long hair with no fringe (bangs), sections from the front can be pinned up to sit high on the crown to balance the tousled look of the longer lengths.

31 When drawing longer hair into a high ponytail, leave a side section free to help frame the face and add some softness to the look.

32 A geometric fringe becomes the focal point when the remaining longer lengths are drawn into a high ponytail at the back of the head.

33 Large sections of hair from the top and front areas of the head are twisted gently before being pinned at the crown to keep hair off the face and create height and style.

30

31

32

33

34

35

36

37

38

39

34 If you want a change from a standard, long ponytail, or need an up-do that's not overly fancy, try wrapping the lengths of the ponytail hair loosely round the tail's base, and pinning in place. Leave side pieces free to be tucked behind the ears for a symmetrical look, which adds individuality and modernity.

35 If you are feeling adventurous, try affixing contrasting coloured hairpieces (called wefts) before piling long hair up to create a truly eye-catching up-do. Remember to keep a sense of balance and proportion when creating up-dos and the results can be simply stunning.

36 Forming long hair into pigtails and curling the lengths is a casual yet pretty look. Parting the hair at the side and smoothing the top section gives a neat finish and provides a contrast to the texture of the pigtails.

37 Afro hair that has been relaxed can look superbly long, sleek and shiny. Use reputable products to take care of the hair and avoid breakage and experiment with different styles. Here a section of front hair has been drawn back over the top of the head to create the illusion of a fringe.

38 With long hair there is plenty of scope to play with contrasting textures. Here, the front section of hair is groomed to look sleek and glossy while the side ponytail is all about texture and volume. It creates a neat yet interesting style.

39 For a cute yet smart look, hair is fixed with a low parting and swept across the forehead to create the suggestion of a fringe where there is none. Pinning up back sections adds height and also introduces an element of texture for an individual touch.

40 It's tricky to dress hair yourself if you're looking for a very structured or detailed up-do. Salons will often happily help for that special occasion. Setting the hair, using padding or hairpieces, a hairdresser can conjure up very special looks to suit your face shape. The addition of hair ornaments, feathers and accessories is where the artistry comes in!

40

Curly hair

Whether you enjoy naturally curly or wavy hair or want to emulate the look when styling your hair, there are plenty of ways to work that curl!

1 Encourage wave with plenty of natural movement by applying styling lotion before rough-drying hair. Pay attention to the roots, which is where you can create volume and lift. It results in a casual yet feminine look.

2 Masses of wave on longer hair can be extremely sumptuous and elegant. Create this look by setting hair on large rollers then breaking up the curl carefully using your fingers and so as to inject superb volume into the style. Use plenty of styling lotion and spray to hold the look all party long.

3 By retaining a sense of shape and defining pieces of hair at the front, a messed-up casual style manages to be both stylish and informal.

4 Lift hair at the roots and rub defining products through the mid-lengths and ends to create maximum impact on naturally very curly hair. The trick is to create plenty of width and volume

5 Wear layered hair in a mass of curls by winding sections of hair round bendy rods and allowing to set before teasing the hair into a fabulous, individual shape. It's all about the oomph! factor.

6 Naturally curly hair still needs to be cut into a shape that allows the curl to spring up nicely and create width and volume at the crown and temple area. Use curl defining products to help style.

7 Straighter hair can be transformed by setting it on rollers or large-barrel tongs. This creates clearly defined, open ringlets, which can be twisted together to exaggerate the curl.

1

2

3

4

5

6

7

8

9

10

11

8 Clearly defined, fat ringlets are a head-turning look. Ensure that flyaways are calmed by using a defining curl product to smooth each ringlet, then spray to hold.

9 Use a large, round brush to create wave and movement on mid-length straight hair, focusing on the ends. Smooth and pin top sections close to the head at ear level for contrast with the wilder, more free-formed curl and to emphasize width and shape.

10 For a seductive look, contrast a long, sweeping and smooth front section with curls on the lower sections by using large-barrelled tongs on the mid-length to ends of the hair. The look to aim for is a wave rather than a curl. Very screen siren.

11 Recreate the über-glamorous look of Hollywood film stars by forming large curls with curling tongs and pinning them at the top of the head. You can work the hair so that curls at the top front are balanced with longer, loose back curls.

12 Don't brush curls as it will break them up too much and make the hair frizzy. Instead, use a wide-toothed comb on the roots to mid-lengths to create shape, then use your fingers to separate curls for better definition.

13 On longer, curly hair with no strong style, a striking choice of colour such as coppery red will provide added impact.

14 For the ultimate screen siren look, form front sections of hair into Marcel waves and spray to hold.

15 Use waves to emphasize an asymmetric hairstyle. Pin up sections of hair to create shape, then tease the ends to make them wispy and almost see-through.

16 Opt for strong waves rather than curl to create a glamorous look that also shows off great condition and superb shine on longer, darker hair.

17 Exaggerating the contrast between smooth sides and a textured, almost quiff-like top area, creates a sophisticated yet funky up-do.

18 Curling tongs can be used to conjure up exuberant volume and movement on very long hair. It's a great way to show off condition and vitality.

19 For a real bedhead look, lightly brush the surface of dry curly hair to create volume and fluffy texture. This works best on shorter curly hair, but be careful not to overdo it!

20 Using a volumizing shampoo and conditioner helps add body to a longer style. Layers cut through will help promote bounce and wave.

21 Even shorter hair can be worn in a curly style provided there is enough length to wrap sections of hair round tongs or bendy rods. The trick is to create volume.

22 Pin up lower sections of hair and grip in place to create a sense of drama with a piled-high shape. Don't make it too formal; keep it looser and fresher.

23 For a soft, stylish look, create a low parting and sweep curls to one side, pinning in place if necessary.

24 For a classic evening look, set hair on large heated rollers then backcomb the roots of the top section to create volume before smoothing over.

18

19

20

21

22

23

24

25

26

25 Longer, curly hair can be twisted and pinned to create this dramatic and rather avant-garde look. This is not a style for the faint-hearted and is more one for the professionals to create rather than something you can try at home! You can use this picture to show them what you want, however. The trick is to use padding or some support to form an exaggerated shape such as this. And plenty of pins and strong-hold spray is required to keep it in place.

26 Use false pieces of curly hair to make a quirky, eye-catching style for a night out. Colour match the pieces with the natural hair, then grip in place underneath your natural hair to conceal the join. When going for an offbeat look such as this, still remember to keep balance and proportion in mind.

27 Arrange luxurious thick hair, either naturally curly or tonged, from a centre parting into a great shape, not forgetting to apply a smoothing and defining product. It's important to keep the hair clean around the face to achieve a groomed rather than dishevelled finished effect.

28 Very tight ringlets worn in a voluminous way from a smooth top section are very dramatic. You can achieve them by setting the hair on pipe-cleaners or even forming tiny plaits (braids) and holding them between straightening irons to set the shape. Remember to set or braid hair leaving a short section of hair near the root free. You can break up underneath sections to enhance the width and volume.

29 Try combing a light gel through damp, clean hair before braiding it and leaving to set and dry. It won't create a strong curl, but will produce waves that can be loosened gently to create a soft, casual look.

30 Working Marcel waves through the front and side sections of a short, one-length bob creates a striking, retro look that complements fine features beautifully. They take time and practice to perfect but are very striking and, once you have the skill, can be versatile, too.

27

28

29

30

31

32

33

34

31 Fringes (bangs) are quite modern looking, so by wearing hair cleanly off your face you instantly evoke a retro vibe. The glorious density of dark hair colour here and the luxurious wave is very filmstar-ish in this wonderful style.

32 Tumbling curls and impeccable, sleek make-up will conjure up memories of the stars of yesteryear. It's a classic, seductive look that works especially well on a special night out. Apply defining crème to bring out the shape of the curl and a generous spritz of shine spray to work the look to the max.

33 A rich dark colour and beautifully conditioned hair looks fantastic when set on rollers and allowed to tumble free, emphasizing shine and a sense of luxury.

34 Large pin curls on longer, blonde hair is so Marilyn Monroe. Set hair, then be very careful not to break up curls when you arrange them to form the desired shape, keeping plenty of height at the forehead and crown.

35 Tonging the free ends of a loose chignon or ponytail is an easy way to give the impression of all-over curls. Use plenty of spray to fix the curls, so they won't drop too quickly.

36 Wearing hair up can look severe, so first tong or set hair to create volume and movement, then pin up sections to create a balanced shape. Allowing tendrils of hair to escape softens the look, too.

37 A true Afro look is exuberant and worked into a fantastic, even balanced shape worn clean off the face.

38 Avoid a severe or too-clean parting, or it can look as though you have tried too hard! A casual parting goes well with gentle curls.

39 Jaw-length Afro hair looks very attractive when it has been cut well so that it has a good shape. It will be easier to control, too.

40 Set mid-length or longer hair on bendy rods, then leave so the curls are more like waves yet remain unbroken, for definition.

35

36

37

38

39

40

BaByliss
BaByliss PRO
BaByliss

Styling tools and techniques

There is a huge range of hairbrushes, combs, accessories, tools, products and heated styling appliances available, and this chapter reveals what they are, how they are used and the options on offer. Once you have the right equipment for your hair, however, you need to master the art of styling it, so here is an invaluable step-by-step guide to some of the basic techniques that will enable you to create an almost endless number of looks – from blow-drying for different finishes to the correct way to use irons and tongs to create curls and waves.

Styling tools

The right tools not only make hairstyling easier, but mean you can be more versatile, too. Hairbrushes, combs and pins are the basic tools of styling and today the choice is enormous. The following is a quick guide to help you choose what is most suitable.

Hairbrushes

A device for detangling, smoothing and shaping hair, a hairbrush comprises bristles (sometimes termed quills or pins), which may be made from natural hog bristle, plastic, nylon or wire, and which are embedded in a wooden, plastic or moulded rubber base and set in tufts or rows. Arranging bristles like this allows loose hair to collect in the grooves without interfering with the action of the bristles moving through your hair. The spacing of the tufts plays an important role – generally, the wider the spacing between the rows of bristles the easier the hairbrush will flow.

The purpose of brushing is to remove tangles and knots and generally smooth the hair. The action of brushing from the roots to the ends removes dead skin cells and dirt, and encourages the cuticles to lie flat, thus reflecting the light. Brushing also stimulates the blood supply to the hair follicles, promoting healthy growth.

Natural bristles are made of natural keratin (the same material as hair) and therefore create less friction and wear on the hair. They are good for grooming and polishing, and help to combat static on flyaway hair. However, they will not easily penetrate wet or thick hair and you must use a softer bristle brush for fine or thinning hair. In addition, the sharp ends can scratch the scalp.

Above *There are many types of brushes to use depending on your choice of style and hair type. Keep several so you are prepared at all times.*

Plastic, nylon or wire bristles are easily cleaned and usually heat-resistant, so they can be used when you are blow-drying, but they may distort if subjected to extreme heat.

▪ Flat or half-round brushes

Ideal for all aspects of wet or dry styling and blow-drying, flat or half-round brushes are good all-round tools but are not precise enough for serious styling, which is where round brushes come in.

Closely set bristles on a flat brush are useful for creating smooth, straight styles where hair isn't long enough to lie easily on the brush. Widely-spaced, thick bristles are ideal for smoothing straight hair which is longer. You can

Far left *A vent brush allows air to move more freely, which is great when blow-drying damp hair to be smooth.*

Left *A flat or paddle brush is useful for styling hair to be smooth and straight. Here, the pins are set in rubber cushioning.*

Far right Use a softer bristle if your hair is prone to breakages or split ends and don't brush too vigorously or you will stress the hair further.

Right A flat-backed brush smoothes hair and is easily drawn through longer styles, making it lie flat.

also use a flat brush to create flicks and movement, drawing the brush through the hair, then turning it out as you reach the ends of the hair.

- **Paddle brushes**

Broad, flat, paddle brushes are great for blow-drying wavy hair to be straight, as well as achieving a poker-straight finish on long hair. Rubber cushioning on the paddle can ensure an extra-smooth, static-free finish.

- **Pneumatic brushes**

These popular brushes have a domed, air-cushioned rubber base with bristles set in tufts. They can be plastic, natural bristle or both and are great for smoothing all types of hair and countering static electricity. The nylon bristles offer more grip for detangling while the natural ones are super-smoothing and perfect for thinner hair.

- **Vent brushes**

Usually made from plastic, vent brushes have vented, hollow centres that allow the airflow from the dryer to pass through them. Special bristle or pin patterns are designed to lift and disentangle even wet hair. Vents and tunnel brush heads enable the air to circulate freely through both the brush and the hair so the hair dries faster.

- **Circular or radial brushes**

These brushes come in a variety of sizes and are circular or semi-circular in shape. Close-set bristles tend to grip the hair more tightly, while widely set bristles will control the air more easily and help remove tangles.

The development of metal or ceramic barrels has been popular as this helps the brush retain heat and better shape the hair (like a roller) when used with a hairdryer. Use these brushes to:

- Tame and control naturally curly, permed and wavy hair.
- Smooth hair during blow-drying; you can draw them through the hair and achieve a smooth finish.
- Create wave or curl when blow-drying – wrapping hair round them and using like a large roller. Leave the brush in the hair as it cools to promote better curl retention.
- Achieve root lift by using the brush to lift the hair away from your head as you blow-dry. The diameter of the barrel of the brush determines the resulting volume and movement: a large diameter creates a soft curl; a smaller one creates a tighter curl. Remember when choosing a radial brush with a large diameter that your hair must be long enough to wrap around it, so don't buy a large brush if you only have short hair.

- **Dressing-out brushes**

These are narrow brushes with only a few rows of bristles set into the head, and they have a tail. They are designed for back-brushing hair at the roots when creating volume and lift, particularly when dressing hair.

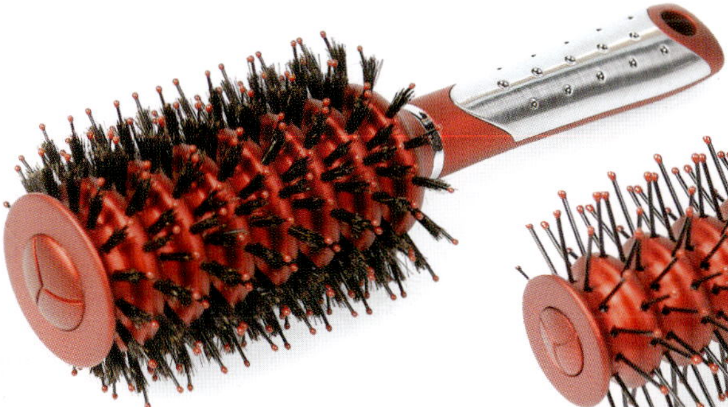

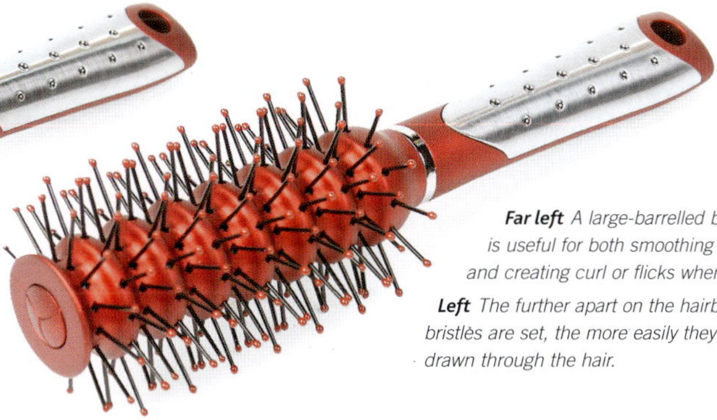

Far left A large-barrelled brush is useful for both smoothing the hair and creating curl or flicks when styling.

Left The further apart on the hairbrush the bristles are set, the more easily they can be drawn through the hair.

Above *Use a comb rather than a brush on damp hair, since it stretches and breaks more easily than dry hair and requires gently care.*

Above *Flat sectioning clips are great for sectioning hair and for using to hold pin curls in place while hair dries.*

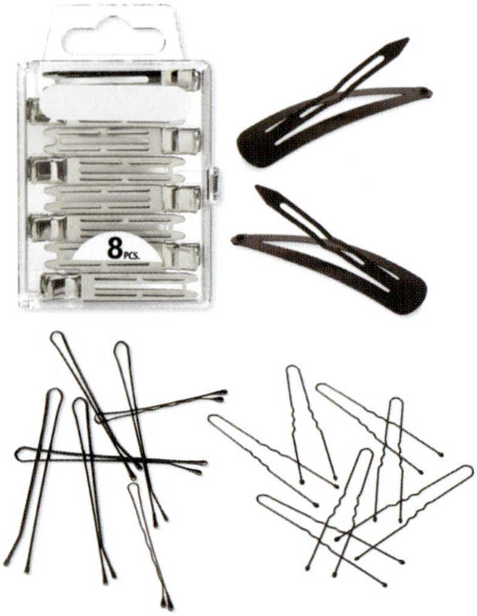

Clockwise, from top left *Small sectioning clips; snap clips; open-ended fine hair pins and hairgrips (bobby pins)*

Combs

Choose good-quality combs with saw-cut teeth. This means that each individual tooth is cut into the comb, so there are no sharp edges. Avoid cheap plastic combs that are made in a mould and so form lines down the centre of every tooth, and replace combs that have damaged teeth. They are sharp, and scrape away the cuticle layers of the hair, causing damage.

- **Wide-toothed combs** are used for disentangling and combing conditioner through the hair.
- **Fine-tail combs** are for styling and sectioning hair. They are the only way to create the perfect parting!
- **Afro combs** are for curly hair as they don't snag as easily.

Pins and clips

Endlessly versatile and cheap, there are several different types to choose from:

- **Open-ended and fine hair pins** are used for securing hair, especially for up-dos such as into chignons. They are quite delicate and prone to bend out of shape, so they should only be used to secure small amounts of hair. These pins are easily concealed, especially if you use a matching colour. They are sometimes used to secure pin curls during setting, rather than heavier clips, which can leave a mark.
- **Twisted pins** are similar to open-ended pins but are fashioned like a screw and are used to secure French pleats (rolls) and chignons.
- **Hairgrips (bobby pins)** are closed hairgrips that lie flat to the head. Prise them apart to slide into the hair and push in as far as possible to help conceal them in the hair. They come in a variety of colours, so choose hairgrips to suit.
- **Sectioning clips** are clips with a double prong that snaps shut, and are longer in length than other clips. They are most often used for holding hair out of the way while working on another section, or for securing pin curls.
- **Snap clips** are stronger and hold more hair than hairgrips but are more difficult to conceal. They snap open so you can pass hair between the outer rim and the inner prong, then snap shut. They are available in different colours.

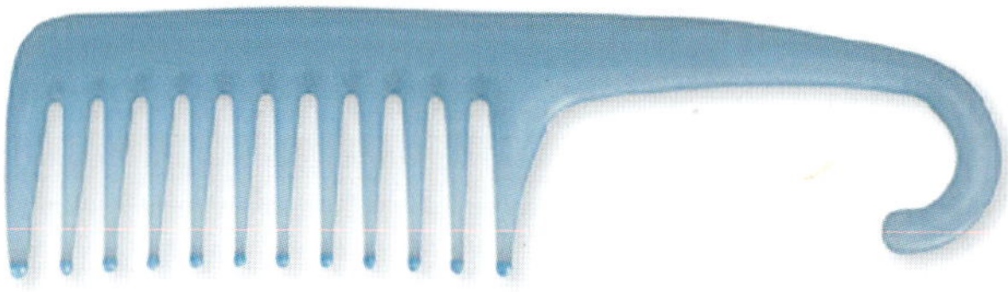

Far top left *A wide-toothed saw-cut comb is a necessity for any hair care regime, especially for detangling wet hair, which can be fragile.*

Far bottom left *Fine combs are an essential tool for getting a professional-looking finish when styling hair.*

Left *Afro combs should be used for very curly hair, for lifting the root area without snagging and tearing hair.*

***Above** Self-gripping rollers do not require clips to hold them in place.*

***Below** Bendable rods are lightweight and covered with foam.*

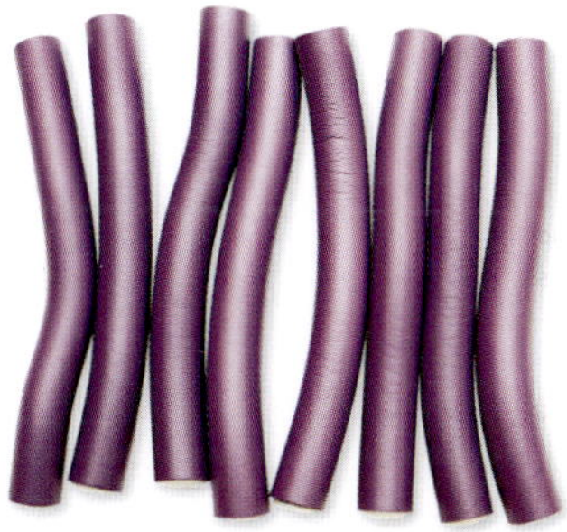

Rollers

Invaluable for creating wave and curl, rollers vary in diameter, length and the material from which they are made:

- **Smooth rollers** do not have spikes or brushes and will give the sleekest finish, but are more difficult to put in.
- **Brush rollers** are more popular, especially the self-holding variety that do not require pins or clips.

Shapers or rods

Producing soft, bouncy curls, shapers or rods are extremely useful pieces of equipment. They were inspired by the principle of rag-rolling hair. Soft 'twist tie' ones are made from pliable rubber, plastic or cotton fabric and provide one of the more natural ways to curl hair. In the centre of each shaper is a tempered wire, which enables it to be bent into shape. The technique is gentle enough for fragile permed or tinted hair.

To use, section clean, dry hair and pull to a firm tension, 'trapping' the end in a shaper that you have previously doubled over. Roll down to the roots of the hair and fold over to secure. Leave in for 30–60 minutes without heat, or for 10–15 minutes if you apply heat. If you twist the hair before curling you will achieve a more voluminous style.

***Below left** Heated rollers are placed in the hair and held in place with bespoke clips, then left to cool.*

***Below** Up-dos often require hair to be set on rollers or curled on tongs to add movement and guts to give shape and volume to the hair.*

Heated appliances

A wide range of gadgets is available for styling your hair quickly and easily, and continuing technological developments mean there are always new and improved products to try. Here's a guide to the main categories and what they do.

Modern technology

Electrical styling tools make great use of a range of different technologies and materials, including:

- **Ionic technology** utilizes negative ions to remove moisture from the hair more quickly. The negative ions break water molecules into smaller particles, which then evaporate faster, cutting drying time. They also help to tighten the hair cuticle, making hair softer and more shiny and reducing frizz.
- **Ceramic heat elements** are great for spreading heat more evenly so you can style hair using a milder heat. Arguably, ceramic plates on irons or tongs are smoother and kinder to the hair than other materials.
- **Far infrared** technology is a new understanding of how to use far infrared rays to help to shorten drying time and reduce damage to the hair from direct heat.
- **Tourmaline** is a mineral compound (similar to ceramic) that emits negative ions and infrared. When incorporated into a dryer design, it can help seal in moisture and dry hair faster. In styling tools, some believe that it produces a smoother, more shiny finish to the hair. Tourmaline and ceramic substances are often combined in the same piece of equipment.

Hairdryers

Used for drying wet hair, hairdryers can also make your hair super-smooth, straight or wavy, add lift and volume.

Narrow nozzles can be fitted on to the end of the hairdryer cylinder and they direct air-flow for precision drying. This is especially useful when smoothing hair. Alternatively, diffuser attachments spread the airflow over the hair to dry it more slowly, with the intention of retaining texture, especially in curly hair, which can become frizzy if you use a standard nozzle.

Travel dryers are ideal for taking on trips and are usually miniature versions of standard dryers. Check you have one with dual voltage. When buying a standard dryer, look out for the following key features:

- A motor of at least 1500 watts (this refers to the power of the motor and how fast it works, decreasing the drying time).
- High- and low-power settings.
- Temperature options and a cool-shot button (for a blast of cold air when you need it).
- Ionic technology, which represents a great step forward in the performance and improved drying times of hairdryers available today.

Drying tips

- Always point the dryer so the air flows down the hair shaft to smooth the cuticle and encourage shine.
- Take care not to hold the dryer too near the scalp; it can cause burns.
- When you have finished blow-drying, allow the hair to cool thoroughly, then check that the hair is completely dry. Warm hair often gives the illusion of dryness while it is, in fact, still damp.
- Never use a dryer without its filter in place – hair can easily be drawn into the machine where it will get caught.

Left to right
Straightening irons; small-barrelled curling tongs; a hairdryer with a nozzle attachment.

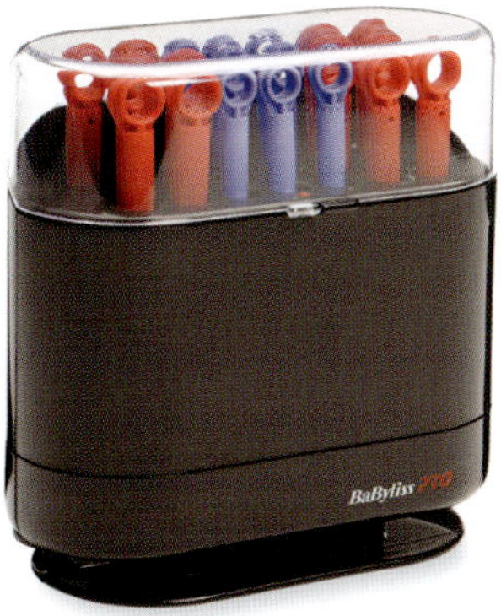

Left *Heated rollers come in many formats, including these upright display rollers.*

Below *Hot sticks are bendable rods that work like small-diameter rollers.*

Straightening irons

Sometimes called flat irons, straightening irons have two heated flat plates which are clamped over a section of hair and slowly drawn to the ends, literally ironing hair as flat and smooth as possible. They can be used to press curly hair, and help tame frizzy hair.

Today, irons are designed with heat controls, either as a digital display unit on the cord or on the iron itself. There is a choice of plate sizes and widths suitable for hair of any length, and they are also available with round-backs, which make it possible to wave the hair (by wrapping sections of hair round the iron before drawing them between the heated plates).

Developments in ionic technology and the use of ceramic plates have improved heat distribution and performance considerably, making irons one of the most versatile styling tools available.

Crimping irons

These irons consist of two ridged, metal plates that are corrugated to produce uniform patterned crimps in straight lines in the hair. Some crimpers have reversible or dual-effect styling plates to give different finishes. Use for special looks or to increase volume. Use only on dry hair that has been spritzed with heat-protective spray to prevent scorching.

Curling tongs

Tongs consist of a barrel, or prong, and a grooved 'depressor' which fits against the barrel and works on a spring action so that hair can be wrapped round the barrel and clamped to hold.

The diameter of the barrel and the size of tong is varied according to the size of curl you want to create and the length of your hair. Use tongs only on dry hair that has been spritzed with heat-protective spray to avoid scorching the hair.

Hot brushes

Looking similar to a curling tong but without the depressor, hot brushes have bristles to grab the hair when wrapping sections to form curls. Hot brushes also come in varying diameters for creating curls of different sizes. Arguably they are best for short to medium length hair and particularly for lifting at the roots.

Heated rollers

Available in sets, heated rollers normally comprise a selection of around 20 small, medium and large rollers, with colour-coded clips of different sizes to match. The early models came with spikes, which many women prefer because they have a good grip, but smooth rollers (held in place with bespoke clips) arguably give a better finish.

New developments include ribbed rubber surfaces, which are designed to be kinder to the hair; curved barrel shapes that follow the form of the head, and clip fasteners.

Hot sticks

Similar to bendable rods or shapers, these are pliable heated sticks that are self-holding (by bending the ends), so no clips are required. Available in ceramic and non-ceramic versions, you place them in the hair when they are hot, twist to fix in place and leave to cool for small, tight curl results.

Styling tips

- Heat-drying encourages static, causing hair to fly away. You can reduce this by smoothing down your hair with your hand.
- With the exception of hairdryers, always use heated electrical styling tools on dry, not wet, hair.
- If you are curling tight up to the roots, try placing a comb between the tongs and the scalp so the comb forms a barrier against the heat and helps to prevent scalp burns.
- Leave tonged curls to cool completely before styling.

Did you know?

- *Only buy electrical equipment from reputable sources and check for a safety standard mark.*
- *Equipment should always be unplugged and put away safely out of reach of children when it is not in use.*
- *Never use electrical equipment with wet hands, and don't use near water.*
- *The cord should not be wrapped tightly around the equipment; coil it loosely before storing safely.*
- *All electrical equipment should be checked periodically to ensure that leads and connections are in good order.*
- *Clean filters regularly – a blocked filter means the dryer has to work harder and will eventually overheat and cut out.*
- *Heat-protective mats are a good idea and now come with many styling tools.*
- *Select products with automatic cut out when left idle. It's no excuse for not switching them off yourself, but could prevent accidents.*

Styling products

Styling and finishing products are designed to help make hair more manageable during the drying and styling process and retain the style longer. They also have conditioning actions to help compensate for the damage done during heat styling.

The combination of practice and the right styling product will enable you to achieve a salon finish at home, so it is worth checking out what does what and how each can help your particular hair type. Many will also be available in a variety of hold strengths, often called hold-factor, ranging from light to extra-firm.

Style it

- **Blow-dry lotions, styling crèmes and sprays** are usually a single-application product that is distributed evenly all over the hair using fingers. They add guts and hold when drying the hair to help maintain the new style. They are similar to leave-in conditioner as they help to limit damage to the hair during styling.
- **Mousse** is the most versatile styling product. It comes as a foam, usually in an aerosol, which makes it easy to distribute, and can be used on wet or dry hair. Mousses contain conditioning agents and proteins to nurture and protect the hair. They are available in different strengths, designed to give soft to maximum holding power, and can be used to lift flat roots or smooth frizz. Use when blow-drying, scrunching and diffuser-drying.
- **Volumizers and thickeners** help plump up flat or lifeless hair. Apply to damp hair before styling and focus on the roots rather than the lengths of the hair. They are often designed for fine hair, so are sold as a light formulation, perhaps as a lotion or light gel.
- **Gels** are styling aids that come in varying degrees of viscosity, from a thick jelly to a liquid spray, but will be heavier than a mousse or a blow-dry lotion. Gels are sometimes called sculpting lotions and are used for precise styling. They can be applied throughout the hair or to specific areas. Use them to lift roots, tame wisps and flyaways, create tendrils, calm static, heat set, and give structure and definition to curls. Wet gel can be used for sculpting styles which then dry to look slick.
- **Curl-activators or hair balms** are used to relax or straighten wavy or curly hair. They will often be delivered in pump-action sprays as light gels, which can then be easily distributed evenly by combing through the hair using a wide-toothed comb. The curl-activators (sometimes called a revitalizer) perk up curls by adding moisture to existing curls, helping renew their bounce.

Right *Different styling products do different things and you may find a blend of several offer the perfect solution for your needs.*

- **Heat-protective sprays and conditioning sprays and creams** should be applied evenly throughout dry hair before using any heated styling tools including heated rollers, straightening irons, curling tongs or crimping irons. They form a barrier to protect the hair from excessive heat and so help prevent it being scorched or damaged.

Finish it

- **Hairspray** is traditionally used to hold a style in place and is available in varying degrees of stiffness to suit all needs. More creative uses include using hairspray to keep the hair in place, get curl definition when scrunching, and to mist over rollers when setting. Flexible or working sprays are also available and allow you to continue moving and shaping the hair after applying.

- **Serums, glossers, polishes and shine sprays** are made from oils or silicones, which improve shine and softness by forming a microscopic film on the surface of the hair. Formulations can vary from light and silky to heavier ones with a distinctly oily feel. They also contain substances designed to smooth the cuticle, encouraging the tiny scales to lie flat and thus reflect the light, and make the hair appear shiny.

Use these products to improve the feel of the hair, to combat static, de-frizz, add shine and gloss, and improve the appearance of split ends. Serum can be mixed with other products for extra-glossy drying or protection.

- **Waxes, pomades and creams** are made from natural waxes, such as carnauba (produced by a Brazilian palm tree), which are softened with other ingredients such as mineral oils and lanolin to make them pliable. They are designed to add definition and hold and both soft and hard formulations are available. Some pomades contain vegetable wax and oil to give gloss and sheen to hair. Other formulations produce foam and are water-soluble, and leave no residue. Use for dressing the hair, creating up-dos and for controlling frizz and static.

Left *Products will be delivered as mousses, sprays, serums, gels and crèmes, depending on how they are to be applied.*

Above *Hairsprays are perfect for fixing an up-do once it is finished, while flexible or working sprays are used during styling.*

Did you know?

- *A light application of hairspray on a hairbrush can be used to tame flyaway ends.*
- *Use hairspray at the roots and tong or blow-dry the area to get immediate lift.*
- *A gel can be revitalized the following day by running wet fingers through the hair, against the direction of the finished look.*
- *If using a styling lotion for heat setting, look out for ones that offer thermal protection.*

Basic styling techniques

There are more ways to style hair than can possibly be outlined in one list, but here is a compilation of the most common techniques that form the basis for many more complex ways of dressing hair. It's all about practice making perfect!

Drying techniques

- **Finger-drying** hair creates gentle informal styles and is a technique that works well when your hair is well-behaved and inclined to fall into a style easily! It's great for drying shorter hair in particular, especially when you're not after a super-smooth finish.

Rather than using combs or brushes, your hands are the styling tools, lifting the hair and moving it in the direction you require, either allowing the hair to dry naturally or using a hairdryer on a low-power setting. You can mould the hair by wrapping it round your fingers, and push it to one side or back off your face.

- **Scrunch drying** is best for achieving fuller, more curly or textured styles on hair that already has some movement – usually medium or longer length. Take damp hair in the palm of your hand and compress it into a curled shape while directing the hairdryer on to the hair and opening and closing your hand to allow the heat into the hair. Keep your hand there until the hair cools and takes on the texture you want.

When the hair is dry and you want to finish the style, continue to scrunch the hair between the fingers and palm, adding styling mousse, gel or wax to help hold the shape.

Above *Using rollers is still arguably the best way to inject lift, volume and curl into hair of all types and lengths.*

- **Natural drying** is a way of giving hair some respite from constant heat-styling. Hair is more elastic when it is wet, and when it is dried using a hairdryer and a brush or comb, the hair is stretched. Elastic recoil is delayed until the next time the hair is wet (either when it is shampooed or moisture is absorbed from the atmosphere). When dried naturally, however, the hair is not put under the duress of stretching, so has time to relax and regenerate.

Setting techniques

This refers to styling hair and putting it into a shape or texture that it doesn't naturally take on. It's a temporary process made possible by the fact that hair will take on moisture, allow itself to be reshaped and then dried or set into this new shape until next time it is dampened.

Left *Heated styling tools need to be used with care as hair is easily scorched and scalps can be burned.*

Setting techniques include curling, straightening, crimping and waving. These are all easily removed by simply washing the hair, returning it to its natural state.

Chemical processing

Sometimes called 'technical services', chemical processing uses chemicals to alter the state of the hair in a permanent or semi-permanent way. Broadly this refers to adding or removing colour, perming for curl, wave or volume, and relaxing to permanently straighten it.

Dressing hair

The art of folding, tying, wrapping and pinning hair into different shapes and designs, without cutting, setting or chemical processing is called dressing. Many styles comprise a technique or a combination of techniques based on the following:

- **Vertical rolls** (also called a pleat, French pleat or thumb roll) are created when hair is drawn off the head and held at a 90 degree angle, then wrapped around itself to form a barrel shape. You can use the fingers or whole hand to create the shape, depending on the size of roll you desire, and this is then pinned vertically against the head. You can form one large roll or use the technique to create smaller rolls.
- **Horizontal rolls** are formed the same way, but are pinned horizontally. They are a great way to accentuate the head shape, especially at the nape, the crown and the forehead.
- **Plaits**, also called braids, are strands of hair woven together. Usually, plaits are three strands of even sizes interwoven, but you can have five strands, and experiment with uneven-width strands.
- **Added hair** refers to wigs and hairpieces, which come in various shapes and sizes and can be made of synthetic fibre, monofibre or real hair. They come on different bases and can be clipped or pinned into your natural hair.
- **Extensions** are made from real or synthetic hair and are fixed or bonded into the root of your natural hair as close to the scalp as possible. They instantly extend the length and are useful for adding volume to fine or thinning hair. They are time-consuming to apply, but will last up to three months.

Common terms

When styling hair, certain parts of the head and neck will be referred to. Here's a guide to exactly where each part is:

- **The nape** is the lowest point of the head, where it joins the central point of the neck.
- **The crown** is the highest point of the head – towards the top back of the skull.
- **The forehead** is the point where hair is furthest forward.
- **The hairline** refers to the line where hair grows on the head.
- **The occipital bone** is the point on the back of the skull that sticks out furthest.

Left *It's tricky to see what's going on at the back when creating styles such as this, so get help with intricate styling and hairdressing,*

Blow-drying shorter hair for a smooth finish

You will need
- Wide-tooth comb
- lightweight holding gel
- Hairdryer
- Nozzle attachment
- Comb
- Paddle brush
- Shine spray

For a really head-turning look that is easy to do, especially on one-length hair (whether short or long), go for a super-sleek finish. It creates shine to bring out the colour of the hair and complements a great head shape.

1 Wash your hair, then towel-dry it to be damp rather than wet. Comb through to detangle using a wide-tooth comb, which won't stretch and break your hair.

2 Apply a lightweight gel and work through your hair using your fingers so it is evenly distributed from roots to ends.

Stylist's note

Light bounces off smooth hair better than textured hair, which is why this finish achieves greater shine.

3 Rough-dry your hair with a hairdryer to be about 80 per cent dry, then style as you like using a comb.

4 Brush your hair from root to end with a paddle brush, following with the hairdryer. Spritz all over with shine spray to finish.

Blow-drying shorter hair smooth with kicked-out ends

Using a brush when blow-drying gives you a super-smooth finish, but remember you can also use it to kick out the ends of the hair. It makes for a refreshing change from straight or curled-under bobbed looks.

You will need

- Wide-tooth comb
- Texturizing product
- Hairdryer
- Nozzle attachment
- Large round brush

Stylist's note

For speed, blow-dry your hair roughly until it is 80 per cent dry before taking more time to smooth the hair by styling with a hairbrush as you finish drying it.

1 Wash your hair, then towel-dry it to be damp. Comb through to detangle using a wide-tooth comb. Apply a texturizer, such as a light-hold gel product.

2 Work the gel through your hair from roots to ends, using your fingers to ensure it is evenly distributed.

3 Rough-dry your hair with a hairdryer, using your fingers to help lift at the roots.

4 Use a large round brush to wrap sections of hair round the bristles, then roll the brush outwards and blast-dry to create a kick at the ends of your hair.

Blow-drying shorter hair for a chic, grown-up look

Short hair doesn't have to be worn close and flat to your head. By using a variety of hairbrushes to lift the hair at the roots as you blow-dry, it's easy to create a smooth yet full-looking style that is neat and chic at the same time.

You will need

- Wide-tooth comb
- Styling spray
- Small-barrelled round brush
- Hairdryer
- Vent brush
- Hairspray

1 Wash your hair, then towel-dry it to be damp rather than wet. Comb through to detangle using a wide-tooth comb, which won't stretch and break your hair.

2 Spritz your hair all over with styling spray to prevent scorching hair when drying it.

Stylist's note

Using a small-barrelled round brush won't necessarily create curl; it can also be used for adding root lift and volume.

3 Blow-dry your hair by wrapping sections round a small-barrelled round brush then lifting and rolling it inwards to achieve smoothness and volume as you dry.

4 Smooth your hair back off your face using a vent brush to create a wedge at the nape of your neck. Spritz with hairspray to finish.

Blow-drying shorter hair for a sleek, shiny finish

Even with dynamic, choppy layers cut into shorter hair, you can still choose to wear a smooth style to accentuate great condition, colour and shape. Use a flat brush to keep hair close to the head and looking sleek.

You will need

- Wide-tooth comb
- Styling lotion
- Hairdryer
- Nozzle attachment
- Flat brush
- Hairspray

1 Wash your hair, then towel-dry it to be damp rather than wet. Comb through to detangle using a wide-tooth comb, which won't stretch and break your hair.

2 Tip some styling lotion into the palm of one hand, then rub your hands together.

Stylist's note

Once styled, you can spritz hairspray on to the hairbrush and run it through your hair to calm flyaways.

3 Rub the styling lotion through the hair using your hands. Ensure it is evenly distributed from root to tip.

4 Blow-dry your hair smooth using a flat brush to keep layers close to the head. Style to show off the cut. Spritz with hairspray to finish.

Blow-drying the perfect long bob

A sleek, swinging bob is a timeless look that never goes out of fashion. Whether yours is cut with or without a fringe, and whatever the length of hair, blow-dry a bob smooth for maximum shine and impact.

You will need

- Wide-tooth comb
- Sectioning clips
- Large round brush
- Hairdryer
- Nozzle attachment
- Shine spray

1 Wash your hair, then towel-dry it to be damp rather than wet. Comb through to detangle using a wide-tooth comb, which won't stretch and break your hair.

2 Section hair from mid-forehead to centre back and across the occipital bone from ear to ear.

3 The back sectioning should now look like this.

4 Starting at the back, place a large, round brush near the roots and hold a dryer with nozzle attachment above the hair.

5 Work round the lower section of your hair before moving to the upper section.

6 Now dry the upper section, continuing to wrap hair round the large round brush for a smooth finish.

7 Blow-dry the fringe (bangs) area using a comb rather than a hairbrush for a smooth but flatter finish.

8 Spritz hair with a light-hold shine spray for a great look.

Stylist's note

This style requires healthy-looking hair, so maintain great condition, and be wary of over-drying, which can cause hair to frizz.

Blow-drying shorter hair for a soft, relaxed look

You will need

- Wide-tooth comb
- Moulding paste
- Hairdryer
- Defining wax
- Shine spray

Giving a shorter haircut a gently dishevelled finish softens a look without making it too sweet or cute. This is an easy-to-achieve and relaxed look that will flatter a strong jawline or a square face shape.

1 Wash your hair, then towel or blow-dry it so it is completely dry.

2 Comb through hair with a wide-tooth comb to eliminate tangles.

3 Put some moulding paste in your palm and rub your hands together, allowing the paste to warm through. This makes it easier to apply.

4 Using your fingers, work the paste through your hair from roots to ends for even coverage and maximum texture and volume.

5 Blast your hair with a hairdryer, focusing particularly on roots for lift and movement.

6 Shake your head and run your fingers through your hair to loosen up the hair.

7 Put some defining wax on your fingertips and rub through pieces of hair to enhance texture.

8 The perimeter of the hair should look shattered, like this. Spritz your hair with shine spray to finish.

Stylist's note

Stiffer products such as moulding pastes are best warmed in the hands to make them more pliable and easier to apply evenly.

Blow-drying shorter hair for a multi-texture effect

Using a combination of straightening irons and styling products you can create a fabulous style that is wearable and striking at the same time. It's fun to play with different textures and contrasts, so let your imagination run wild.

You will need

- Hairbrush
- Comb
- Heat-protective spray
- Straightening irons
- Hairspray

1 Brush clean, dry hair to be tangle-free, then put it in a diagonal front parting, as shown.

2 Comb through the front section so it is really smooth.

3 Spritz your hair all over with heat-protective spray to prevent scorching hair when straightening it.

4 Apply straightening irons through the front section, working from the roots to the ends, to make it as smooth as possible.

5 Taking one small section at a time from the rest of your hair, twist the hair upwards with your fingers.

6 Clamp the twist between the plates of the straightening irons, hold for 5 seconds and release.

7 Continue to work small sections over the whole head in the same way, but always leaving out the smooth front section.

8 Using the fingers, loosen the twists slightly so they blend together, then spritz all over with hairspray for hold.

Stylist's note

Clamping twists of hair in the straightening irons ensures that the texture will remain fixed until you wash it out.

Blow-drying shorter hair for a textured finish

You will need

- Wide-tooth comb
- Texturizing product
- Hairdryer
- Nozzle attachment
- Flexible or working spray

When time is of the essence, working with the natural texture and movement of shorter hair is a fast way to achieve a great look that will appear to have taken longer to create than it really has. Fantastic!

1 Wash your hair, then towel-dry it to be damp rather than wet. Comb through to detangle using a wide-tooth comb, which won't stretch and break your hair.

2 Apply a texturizing product to your hair and evenly distribute it through using your fingers. The thicker the product, the more textured the hair will appear.

Stylist's note

Invest in an ionic hairdryer, which won't suck all the moisture out of the hair, leaving it in better condition and reducing static and frizz.

3 Holding the hairdryer at least 6cm/2½in away from your hair (to avoid scorching), blast-dry, using your fingers to keep shaping the hair and to prevent tangles forming.

4 Spritz your hair with a flexible spray, sometimes called a working spray, which offers some hold without preventing movement.

Blow-drying to add contrast to a shorter textured style

Working smooth sections into a textured hairstyle can be very striking and create an individual finish that is fun yet smart or chic at the same time. Use a shine spray to emphasize the contrast between the smooth and more choppy textures.

You will need

- Comb
- Styling mousse
- Hairdryer
- Nozzle attachment
- Flat brush
- Smoothing crème
- Hairspray

1 Wash your hair, then towel-dry it to be damp rather than wet. Comb through to detangle. Apply styling mousse throughout, using your fingers and ensuring it is evenly distributed.

2 Rough-dry the main part of your hair with a hairdryer, using your fingers to achieve maximum texture and movement.

3 Smooth out the front section by blow-drying it, using a flat brush to emphasize different layers in the hair.

4 Sweep the front section to one side, slick on a small amount of smoothing crème and spritz with light-hold spray to fix hair in position.

Stylist's note

For a smoother back area and more choppy front, simply reverse the process, always using the fingers to create texture where you want it, but working hair around a brush for sleeker finishes.

Blow-drying to add volume and choppy texture to shorter hair

A choppy finish to a short haircut instantly adds individuality to your look. Make the style as exuberant as you like and emphasize layers and colours in the hair by applying a wax or defining spray and shaping with your fingers.

You will need

- Wide-tooth comb
- Light-hold gel
- Hairdryer
- Nozzle attachment
- Medium-hold hairspray
- Defining wax

1 Wash your hair, then towel-dry it to be damp. Detangle using a wide-tooth comb, which won't stretch and break your hair. Squeeze some light-hold gel into the palm of your hand.

2 Massage the gel into your hair using your fingers, ensuring it is distributed evenly from root to tip.

3 Rough-dry your hair using a hairdryer, lifting the hair to direct heat specifically at the roots.

4 Spray the roots with a medium-hold hairspray for height, volume and staying power. Apply a defining wax to finish, piecing it through the ends to add definition.

Stylist's note

A heavily textured finish is a fantastic way to bring out the different highlights in your hair.

Blow-drying mid-length hair for all-over texture

You will need

- Wide-tooth comb
- Texturizing spray
- Hairdryer
- Nozzle attachment
- Small-barrelled round brush
- Hairspray

Creating texture all over your hair doesn't mean going wild. Use a small-barrelled round brush to imbue your hair with movement and softness that is smart-looking yet relaxed too, and which won't look as though you've tried so hard.

1 Wash your hair, then towel-dry it to be damp rather than wet. Comb through to detangle using a wide-tooth comb, which won't stretch and break your hair.

2 Spritz your hair with texturizing spray directed at the roots for lift and then at the mid-lengths to add volume.

Stylist's note

Break up a blocky fringe (bangs) by sweeping it to one side, or pushing it up, and blast-drying the roots with a hairdryer for height and hold.

3 Rough-dry the hair with a hairdryer, then work round the head wrapping irregular sections of hair round a small-barrelled round brush and drying into shape.

4 Style your hair as you like, then spritz with hairspray to hold.

Blow-drying fringed mid-length hair for a textured finish

Have a little fun and create a vibrant, natural look with movement and style that brings out your individuality. Contrasting a smooth fringe with the rest of the hair prevents this look from becoming too casual.

You will need

- Wide-tooth comb
- Texturizing styling spray
- Hairdryer
- Nozzle attachment
- Hairbrush

1 Wash your hair, then towel-dry it to be damp rather than wet. Comb through to detangle using a wide-tooth comb, which won't stretch and break your hair.

2 Spritz a texturizing spray on the roots of your hair to help create lift when drying.

Stylist's note

There are plenty of great texturizing products that you can experiment with. A spray is easy to apply, especially when you are focusing on one area in particular.

3 Blast-dry your hair with a hairdryer, directing heat at the roots to create volume and using your fingers to lift your hair for a less polished finish.

4 Wrap the fringe (bangs) area round a hairbrush and blow-dry it smooth for contrast with the rest of your hair.

Blow-drying mid-length or longer hair for a loose finish

Use this simple technique to achieve a clean, natural finish that doesn't look forced or overdone. Quick and easy to do, it will enable you to be ready and heading for the door super-quickly, safe in the knowledge that your hair looks amazing.

You will need

- Wide-tooth comb
- Smoothing product
- Hairdryer
- Nozzle attachment
- Light-hold shine spray

1 Wash your hair, then towel-dry it to be damp rather than wet. Comb through to detangle using a wide-tooth comb, which won't stretch and break your hair.

2 Apply a smoothing product such as a light balm to your hair using your fingers, paying particular attention to the mid-lengths and ends rather than the roots.

Stylist's note

Point the hairdryer so the warm air only flows down the length of the hair, helping smooth the cuticles to create shine.

3 Holding the dryer at least 6cm/2½in away from your hair (to avoid scorching), dry the hair, running your fingers through the lengths to prevent tangles forming.

4 Apply a light-hold shine spray all over to finish.

Blow-drying mid-length or longer hair to curl under

A neat, classic finish that works best on longer or mid-length hair that has either no layers or just simple graduation, this is a perfect wear-anywhere style that will take you from home to the office and on to the dance-floor, looking good every time.

You will need

- Wide-tooth comb
- Styling serum
- Sectioning clips
- Large round brush
- Hairdryer
- Nozzle attachment

Stylist's note

Using a large round brush to finish the styling achieves a better curl than a flatter brush can.

1 Wash your hair, then towel-dry it to be damp rather than wet. Comb through to detangle using a wide-tooth comb, which won't stretch and break your hair.

2 Put some styling serum in the palm of one hand, then rub your hands together.

3 Rub the serum through your hair from root to tip, distributing the product evenly. Section off one side, twisting and clipping it out of the way with sectioning clips until needed.

4 Take sections of hair and wrap around a large round brush, turning it under. Blow-dry. Repeat to dry all the hair.

Blow-drying mid-length or longer hair for a bedhead finish

Shake up your style by moving away from the groomed look and instead adding as much texture as possible to your hair's natural movement. This works particularly well for shorter or mid-length cuts that have some layering.

You will need

- Wide-tooth comb
- Volumizing mousse
- Hairdryer
- Hairspray

1 Wash your hair, then towel-dry it to be damp rather than wet. Comb through to detangle using a wide tooth comb, which won't stretch and break your hair.

2 Squirt some volumizing mousse into the palm of your hand and apply it liberally throughout the hair for body and volume. Ensure it is evenly distributed from root to tip.

Stylist's note

Avoid creating 'holes' in the style by keeping the hairdryer moving and not lingering too long on one spot.

3 Blast-dry the hair by continually moving the hairdryer swiftly around the head but focusing particularly on the roots to add lift.

4 Scrunch the hair between your fingers and palm to add texture and lift as the hair dries. Spritz all over with hairspray to hold the style.

Blow-drying longer hair for a smooth finish

Long hair looks sensational when it moves with a shiny, healthy swing, so take a little more time than usual when blow-drying to maximize a sleek finish. It's well worth the effort, and is easier than you think to achieve.

You will need

- Wide-tooth comb
- Styling mousse
- Sectioning clips
- Bristle brush
- Hairdryer
- Nozzle attachment
- Shine spray

1 Wash your hair, then towel-dry it to be damp rather than wet. Comb through to detangle using a wide-tooth comb, which won't stretch and break your hair.

2 Squirt some mousse into the palm of your hand, then rub your hands together and apply the mousse to the mid-lengths and ends of your hair.

3 Section the hair, twisting and clipping the upper and side pieces out of the way with sectioning clips. Ensure the front parting is where you will want it to be when you finish blow-drying the hair.

4 When the hair has been sectioned, the back of your head should look like this, with the hair at the back ready to be dried first.

5 Starting at the back, place a bristle brush near the roots and hold a hairdryer so the nozzle points down along the length of the hair.

6 Keep drawing the brush through the section of hair, following with the hairdryer, holding it at least 6cm/2in from the hair to prevent scorching.

7 When the back is dry, work around the sides of the head, drying one section at a time in the same way.

8 When all the hair is dry and smooth, spritz all over with a light shine spray to finish.

Stylist's note

Using sectioning clips makes it easier to work through the hair systematically and achieve a professional-looking finish.

Blow-drying longer hair for volume and movement

Fixing a diffuser attachment onto the hairdryer is a great way to achieve volume and natural texture on longer hair. Easy to achieve, this technique is a gentle way to enhance fullness and movement for a luxurious, head-turning finish.

You will need

- Wide-tooth comb
- Heat-protective spray
- Sectioning clips
- Hairdryer
- Diffuser attachment

1 Wash your hair, then towel-dry it to be damp rather than wet. Comb through to detangle using a wide-tooth comb, which won't stretch and break your hair.

2 Spritz your hair all over with a heat-protective spray to prevent scorching hair when drying it.

3 Section off the top area, twisting and clipping it out of the way with sectioning clips until needed.

4 Fix the diffuser attachment to the end of the hairdryer.

5 Position the diffuser under the ends and mid-lengths of your hair (it can touch the hair) and select a cool- to mid-heat temperature.

6 Work around your head drying your hair in sections, ensuring it rests on the diffuser, to help maximize texture.

7 When you have finished the lower sections should have plenty of texture and volume.

8 Remove the sectioning clips and work through the top section of hair in the same way, until all your hair is completely dry.

Stylist's note

Use a gentle heat-setting on the hairdryer and take time to really get the best finish without hair becoming frizzy.

Blow-drying curly hair for a soft, smooth look

It's possible to achieve a smooth look even on naturally very curly hair. Use your expertise with blow-drying to straighten the hair, then tame movement using straightening irons and styling products for a fantastic finish.

You will need

- Wide-tooth comb
- Styling lotion
- Sectioning clips
- Hairdryer
- Nozzle attachment
- Large-barrelled brush
- Heat-protective spray
- Comb
- Straightening irons
- Serum
- Shine spray

1 Wash your hair, then towel-dry it to be damp. Comb through to detangle using a wide-tooth comb, which won't stretch and break your hair. Apply styling lotion hair using your fingers to ensure it is distributed evenly from root to end.

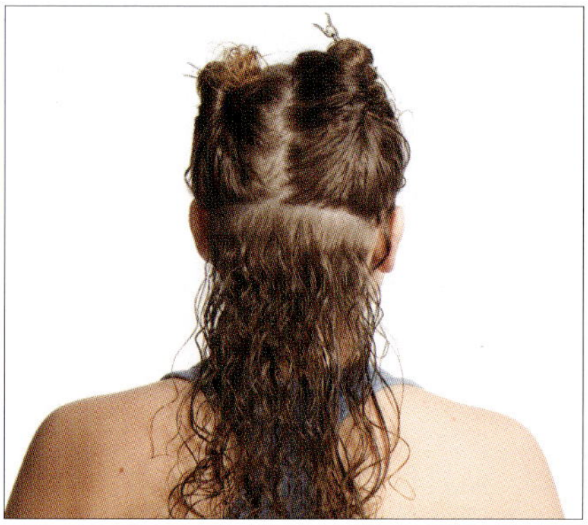

2 Section your hair into three parts using sectioning clips, as shown. This will make drying and straightening your hair easier.

3 Working through the sections, blow-dry the hair by wrapping it round a large-barrelled brush to achieve as smooth a finish as possible

4 Spritz your hair all over with heat-protective spray.

5 Section your hair again into three parts. Comb your hair to ensure it is tangle-free.

6 Apply straightening irons to each section in turn, working from root to end .

7 Apply shine spray and serum to your hair for a super-sleek finish.

Stylist's note

Don't cut corners by skipping the smooth blow-dry as part of this technique. Applying straightening irons to curly hair just won't deliver a sleek result.

Blow-drying to add emphasis to a deep, wide fringe

Accentuating a strong or noticeable feature of a haircut, such as a deep fringe, creates a striking look. Contrast the texture of the fringe with the rest of your hair to create emphasis, using different styling products and tools.

You will need

- Wide-tooth comb
- Styling mousse
- Hairdryer
- Nozzle attachment
- Small-barrelled round brush
- Hairspray

1 Wash your hair, then towel-dry it to be damp rather than wet. Comb through to detangle. Apply styling mousse throughout, using your fingers and ensuring it is evenly distributed.

2 Blow-dry your hair, continually working the hair by scrunching it up between your palm and fingers to create texture.

Stylist's note

To apply hairspray, hold the can above your head so that the spray settles on to your hair as it falls.

3 Dry the fringe (bangs) area smooth by wrapping the hair round a small-barrelled brush and brushing downwards, lifting the hair as you go, while drying.

4 Spritz hair with a light-hold spray to finish and smooth the front section using the palm of the hand to calm flyaways.

Tonging shorter hair for texture

You will need

- Heat-protective spray
- Small-barrelled tongs
- Styling wax

For a more groomed yet texturized finish that doesn't involve rough-drying or back-combing, then practise using tongs. As long as there is enough length to wrap hair once around the barrel then you can achieve a great look this way.

1 Spritz dry, clean hair all over with heat-protective spray to prevent scorching hair when tonging it.

2 Taking one small section of hair at a time, place the tongs at the end of the hair and wind up to the roots. Hold for a few seconds.

Stylist's note

If sections of your hair are too short to wrap around the tongs, leave this hair free and work with longer sections only.

3 This technique forms small half-curls, as shown. Work around the entire head in the same way, including a fringe (bangs) area.

4 To finish, gently loosen the curls with your fingers (not a hairbrush) and apply a small amount of styling wax to separate and define the texture.

Using tongs for different curled effects

You will need
- Comb
- Heat-protective spray
- Curling tongs
- Hairspray

Practise using curling tongs in different ways to create all types of curl, including ringlets and spiral winds. Tongs are a fantastically versatile styling tool once you have the know-how and you can choose ones with different-size barrels to suit.

1 Comb through clean, dry hair so that it is tangle-free.

2 Spritz your hair all over with a heat-protective spray to prevent the tongs from scorching or drying out your hair.

3 Working with a small section of hair at a time, place the tongs at the end and wind back up to the root. Hold for a few seconds, then release. Repeat the action with all of your hair.

4 Alternatively, for a softer curl, place the tongs near the root and wrap the hair round the barrel of the tongs until you reach the end.

5 For a spiral wind, using small-barrelled tongs, take smaller sections of hair and wind from the ends up to the roots while holding the tongs vertically.

6 This is how a spiral wind finish looks when it has been applied to the whole head.

7 When all your hair is curled as you want it, tip your head upside down and shake to loosen curls.

8 If desired, loosen again by running your fingers through the hair, then spritz with hairspray for hold.

Stylist's note

For a strong curl, wind the tongs from end to root, but for a softer look, roll from root to end.

Using tongs to create random spiral curls

You will need

- Heat-protective spray
- Curling tongs
- Hairspray

Rather than creating an all-over curl, tong individual sections of hair then wrap the curled hair around pieces of loose, straighter hair. This is a different take on a classic look and is a great way of ringing the changes!

Stylist's note

Tongs come in different-size barrels, so the shorter the hair, the smaller the barrel-size of tong you need to use.

1 Comb through clean, dry hair so that it is tangle-free. Spritz your hair all over with a heat-protective spray to prevent it from scorching or drying out your hair.

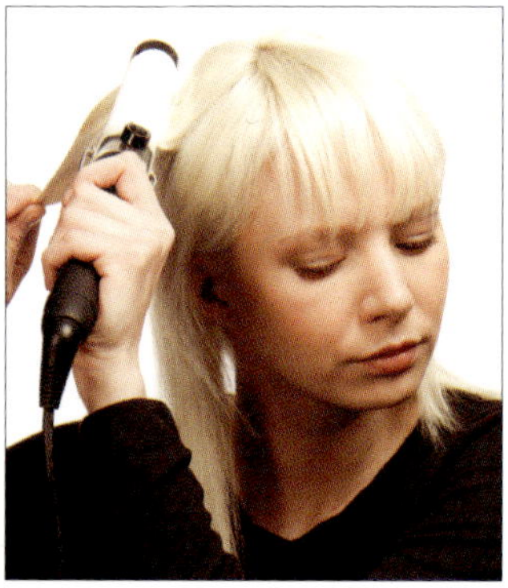

2 Taking a small section of hair, place the tongs near the root and clamp shut.

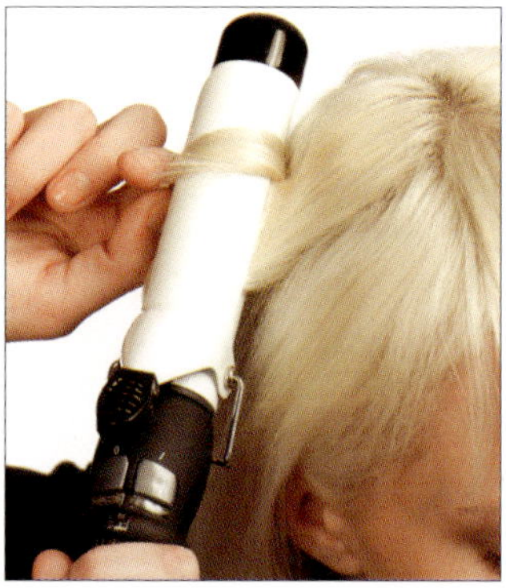

3 Wind the section of hair round the barrel of the tong, working down to the end. Winding this way adds volume and shape.

4 Work random sections of hair in the same way. Finished spirals can be wound around a straight section of hair. Spritz with hairspray for hold.

Using tongs to create all-over curl

A fabulous head of curls is so striking and elegant and makes hair look thicker and more luxurious. Tonging hair will bring out the layers and shape already cut into the hair and, if styled and finished carefully, will stay in as long as needed.

You will need

- Heat-protective spray
- Curling tongs
- Hairspray

1 Comb dry hair to be tangle-free then spritz all over with a heat-protective spray to prevent it from scorching.

2 Working a small section of hair at a time, place the hot curling tongs in your hair near the roots and wind the hair around the tongs from root to end.

Stylist's note

Taking small sections of hair at a time and ensuring the tongs are always well-heated helps achieve an even curl.

3 Hold the tongs closed for several seconds, allowing the heat to penetrate and set curl into the hair.

4 Continue to tong all the hair in the same way. Allow curls to cool before loosening with your fingers. Spritz with hairspray to hold.

Using irons to create striking blades in shorter hair

This strong look is great fun for girls who dare to be different. It takes time to achieve but will last well throughout the day or evening. The added zig-zag texture keeps it individual and prevents the look becoming too futuristic.

You will need

- Hairbrush
- Strong-hold hairspray
- Straightening irons
- Open-ended pins

1 Brush clean, dry hair to be completely tangle-free.

2 Spritz your hair generously all over with a strong-hold hairspray.

3 Working with very small sections of hair at a time, place the straightening irons near the root, clamp shut and draw through the hair from root to end. Repeat with all your hair.

4 Straightened sections must not be brushed or combed, as this would make them separate. Allow them to cool as individual mini blades of hair.

5 Work the whole head in the same way until all hair has been styled into blades.

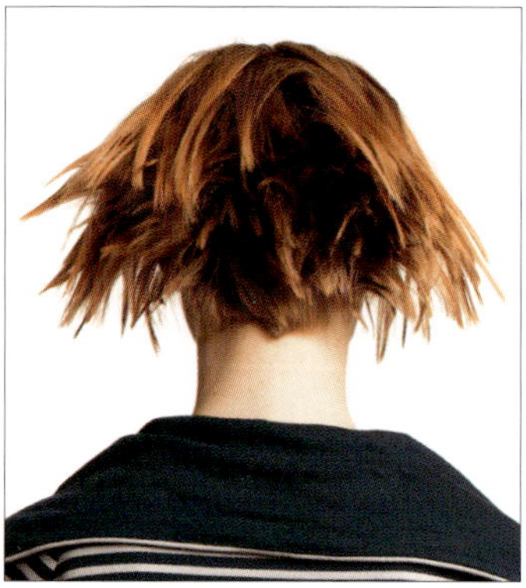

6 Your hair should look like this from the back when you have finished.

7 Taking long, open-ended pins, wind random blades around the prongs of a pin into an 'S'-shape, as shown.

8 Clamp each pin between hot straightening irons for a few seconds, then release and allow to cool before unwrapping the hair. The hair will now have a zigzag detail, as shown.

Stylist's note

Using a hairspray instead of a heat-protective spray for this style gives extra holding power while still protecting hair from scorching.

Using irons to create movement in shorter hair

Hot straightening irons can be used in many ways, not just to smooth but also to wave hair or to add volume and create movement. It's fun to try different-sized irons, and irons with half-round plates to achieve different finished effects.

You will need

- Comb
- Heat-protective spray
- Straightening irons
- Hairspray

Stylist's note

Some irons have more of a barrel shape, which is useful for creating movement and a more textured finish.

1 Comb dry hair to be tangle-free then spritz all over with a heat-protective spray to prevent it from scorching.

2 Taking a small section of hair, place the straightening irons near the root, clamp shut and draw through the hair, turning the irons slightly to create a bend in the hair.

3 Continue applying the irons around the head, working all the hair that is long enough to be shaped in the same way.

4 Rake through your hair with your fingers to loosen and soften the look. Shape as desired and spritz with hairspray to finish.

7 This picture shows the contrast between hair that has been ironed and hair that has not.

8 When all the hair is ironed, spritz all over with shine spray to finish.

Stylist's note

Use a heat-protective spray after drying and before straightening to help keep hair healthy.

Using irons to create movement in longer hair

It's fun to accentuate the layers and longer length of hair by applying straightening irons in such as a way as to add waves and movement. It's also a great way for making hair appear thicker and is less severe than poker-straight hair.

You will need

- Wide-tooth comb
- Styling lotion
- Sectioning clips
- Hairbrush
- Hairdryer
- Hairdryer
- Straightening irons
- Hairspray

1 Wash your hair, then towel-dry it to be damp rather than wet. Comb through to detangle using a wide-tooth comb, which won't stretch and break your hair.

2 Rub a styling product or lotion through your hair so it will retain its shape better when it is dry.

3 Section off the top area of your hair with sectioning clips.

4 Starting with the lower layers, take one small section of hair at a time, wrap it around a brush and blow-dry to give a smooth finish.

5 When all your hair is completely dry, section off the top area again and clip it out of the way.

6 Taking a small section of hair from underneath, place the straightening irons near the root, clamp shut and draw through the hair, flicking the ends out.

7 Continue around your head and through the top section until all of your hair is flicked out at the ends.

8 Spritz your hair with a light to medium-hold spray, focusing on spritzing the ends from underneath to encourage the kick.

Stylist's note

It's important to blow-dry hair properly before applying irons to create the movement or the style will drop quickly.

Crimping loose hair for all-over texture

You will need

- Comb or hairbrush
- Heat-protective spray
- Sectioning clips
- Crimping irons
- Hairspray

Crimping your hair is always a fantastic way to really plump up fine or flat hair or add texture and volume for when you want to wear you hair up. The secret is to not crimp too close to the roots or your style will balloon!

1 Brush dry hair to be completely tangle-free and smooth.

2 Spritz your hair all over with a heat-protective spray to prevent it from scorching or drying out your hair.

3 Section off the top area of hair on either side of the parting with a comb and clip it out of the way using sectioning clips.

4 Starting with the underneath section, apply hot crimping irons to one small section at a time. Hold closed for 3 seconds. Repeat, working down the length of the hair.

5 Work all the underneath hair before moving on to the top section. Ensure crimps are placed evenly or the result will look odd.

6 Crimped hair should look like this when you have finished.

7 Loosen the crimps by running your fingers through your hair.

8 Tease sections of hair to create volume and a softer, more angel-hair finish. Spray with hairspray to hold.

Stylist's note

Remember to carefully position the irons to form an even crimp pattern down each length of hair.

Crimping dressed hair for partial texture

You will need

- Comb
- Hairband (headband)
- Heat-protective spray
- Crimping irons

You can have fun and add crimps to your hair without committing to an all-over crimped finish. Decide first how to dress your finished hair to show off the textured areas, then select sections of hair to crimp, creating a style that works for you.

1 Comb dry hair smooth. Secure in a ponytail at the back of the head with a hairband (headband), leaving some front hair free. Spritz loose hair with heat-protective spray

2 Starting with the loose front section, clamp the crimping irons on the chosen area – starting near the top but not too near the root. Hold for a few seconds.

Stylist's note

If you have fine hair, be careful not to hold the crimping irons closed for too long or you risk scorching your hair. Ensure you always apply heat-protective spray before using crimping irons.

3 Release the irons but do not brush your hair as this will cause the crimped area to frizz. Leave hair to cool.

4 Select random sections of the ponytail, spritz with heat-protective spray and repeat the crimping action.

Crimping loose hair for a random texture effect

For a loose, fresh style that is easy to achieve, crimp random sections of hair as shown opposite, but leave it to hang loose. This technique works well on mid-length to longer hair, adding interest without too much volume.

You will need

- Comb
- Hairband (headband)
- Heat-protective spray
- Crimping irons
- Light-hold hairspray

1 Follow the technique shown opposite up to Step 3, then remove the hairband (headband). Shake your hair free but do not brush it.

2 Generously spritz your hair all over with a light-hold spray to add more volume and to ensure the style will hold.

Stylist's note

Crimping shorter hair can add too much width, which is very hard to balance in a style, so it is advisable to use crimps only if you have mid-length or longer hair.

3 Apply the crimping irons to random sections of hair that have not yet been worked, especially at the top and back of the head, and hold for a few seconds.

4 Loosen the hair using your fingers to break up the crimped sections slightly and to add extra volume and movement to the style.

Setting hair on heated rollers

Using heated rollers means you can multi-task while getting ready! The hair can be set on rollers and you can then move around and continue dressing and applying make-up until the rollers have cooled and are ready for removing.

You will need

- Heated rollers
- Styling lotion
- Sectioning clips
- Pins
- Hairspray

1 Plug in the heated rollers. Apply styling lotion liberally to dry, detangled hair. Section off the top-back area and start working the lower and front areas of hair first.

2 Taking small sections of hair from these lower and front areas, wind the pre-heated rollers from end to root and use pins to hold them in place.

Stylist's note

A set of heated rollers will include a variety different-sized rollers. Put larger ones through the top sections to create lift and movement.

3 Working through all the hair, including the sectioned-off top section, wrap all your hair in rollers and leave to cool completely – about 30 minutes.

4 Remove the rollers and loosen the curls using your fingers. Pin up random sections to create an individual style. Spritz with hairspray.

Setting hair on self-gripping rollers

For a softer set or for when heated rollers are not an option, use rollers that stay in all on their own. Lightweight and available in different sizes, they are perfect for hair that curls quickly and easily, and they are comfortable to use, too.

You will need

- Wide-tooth comb
- Styling lotion
- Self-gripping rollers
- Hairspray

1 Wash your hair, then towel-dry it to be damp rather than wet. Comb through to detangle using a wide-tooth comb, which won't stretch and break your hair.

2 Spritz your hair all over with styling lotion to help set and hold the style.

Stylist's note

Self-gripping rollers are a fantastic way of curling hair when you are on holiday as they are easy and light to pack and don't need to be heated.

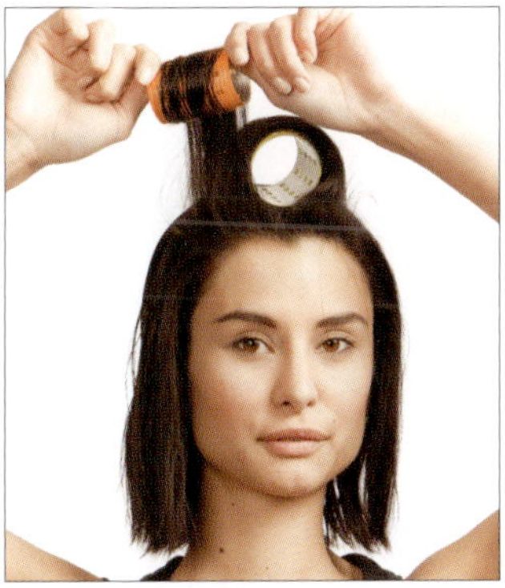

3 Taking one small section of hair at time and starting at the top of your head, wrap hair around the rollers, working from the end to the root. Repeat with all your hair.

4 Allow hair to dry naturally (or apply a gentle heat using a hairdryer). Remove the rollers, loosen your hair with your fingers and spray to hold.

Using bendable rods to create an even curl

Using long fabric or plastic bendable rods is a great way to create even, tight curls. Wound into damp hair, they can then be left to dry naturally. This is a gentle curling technique that is ideal for more fragile colour-treated or even permed hair.

You will need

- Wide-tooth comb
- Light gel-based product
- Sectioning clips
- Bendable rods
- Hairdryer
- Finishing spray
- Pins

1 Wash your hair, then towel-dry it to be just damp. Comb through to detangle using a wide-tooth comb. Apply a light gel-based styling product and work through the hair from root to end.

2 Section your hair into manageable working sections using sectioning clips, twisting the hair and clipping it out of the way so that it doesn't dry out while you are positioning the rods.

3 Taking a small section of hair, place a rod near the end and wind up to the roots. Bend the ends of the rod inwards to hold it in place.

4 Repeat the technique and place rods all around the head, working section by section.

5 When all the hair is wound and all the rods are bent into position, your head should look like this. Allow hair to dry naturally.

6 Remove the rods by unbending them and gently pulling them out, working systematically through the hair.

7 Loosen the curls by lightly running your fingers through them. Do not use a hairbrush as this can create frizz.

8 Spritz your hair all over with finishing spray for hold. To create shape, pin up random sections as preferred.

Stylist's note

As with all curling methods, the smaller the diameter of the rod, the tighter the curl will be.

Using pin curls to create a gentle, tumbling curl

This is a handy technique for creating curls overnight as pin curls are much more comfortable to sleep in than rollers. It is also perfect for when you are on the move as a pack of pins takes up very little room in a suitcase.

You will need

- Wide-tooth comb
- Styling lotion
- Hairgrips (bobby pins)
- Hairdryer

1 Comb dry hair to be tangle-free and spritz all over with a styling lotion to help hold the curl.

2 Working with one small section at a time, wrap pieces of hair round your fingers, as though winding on a roller, to form a curl shape.

Stylist's note

The smaller the sections of hair pinned in place and the longer they are left in to set, the curlier the finished look will be.

3 Lay the curl flat against your head and grip it in place with one pin, or two pins crossed if you require extra hold.

4 When all the hair is pinned, apply heat or leave overnight. Remove the pins and finger-comb your hair, then style.

Using barrel curls to create volume and soft curl

For a look that's reminiscent of a natural wave or curl and which looks just as glamorous and stylish, practise this simple technique for barrel curls. It produces a gentle, soft, cascading curl effect.

You will need

- Wide-tooth comb
- Styling lotion
- Hairgrips (bobby pins) or clips
- Light-hold shine spray

Stylist's note

To speed up the set, dry hair with a hairdryer but use a low heat-setting to avoid blasting the barrel curls out of shape.

1 Wash your hair, then towel-dry it to be damp rather than wet. Comb through to detangle using a wide-tooth comb. Apply styling lotion generously throughout the hair.

2 Taking a small section of hair at a time, wrap the hair loosely round your fingers to create a barrel shape, or large loop.

3 Use a hairgrip (bobby pin) or clip to secure the curl to your head, as shown, then continue to work the remaining hair into curls in the same way.

4 Allow your hair to dry. Remove the hairgrips and loosen the curl using your fingers or by brushing. Spritz with a shine spray.

Using plaits to create a gentle wave

By simply braiding hair into plaits and leaving it for a few hours, you can add a great-looking gentle wave and movement into any hair type. It's a handy method that can be adapted for keeping hair tidy then later revealing a great style.

You will need

- Hairbrush
- Sectioning clips
- Hairspray
- Hairbands (headbands)
- Shine spray

Stylist's note

The tighter you weave the plaits, the more pronounced the wave will be.

1 Brush dry hair until it is smooth and tangle-free.

2 Section your hair down the centre back of the head. Clip one half out of the way, then liberally spritz loose hair with hairspray for hold.

3 Divide this loose hair into three equal strands and weave them into a loose plait (braid), securing the end with a hairband (headband). Repeat on the other side.

4 Leave for a few hours, then untie the plaits and run your hands through to loosen. Spritz with shine spray to finish.

Using multi-plaits to create a stonger wave

Braiding hair into several plaits will accentuate any natural wave in the hair. You can decide how many plaits you need, depending on how thick your hair is. However many you need, make sure they are similar-sized for an even finish.

You will need

- Comb
- Styling lotion
- Sectioning clips
- Hairbands (headbands)
- Hairdryer
- Hairspray

1 Comb through damp hair. Apply styling lotion throughout, then section your hair into a minimum of four similar-sized sections. Make more if you want a more textured finish.

2 Work through each section in turn, weaving the hair into plaits (braids) and securing the ends with hairbands (headbands).

Stylist's note

Starting with damp hair and leaving hair to dry overnight gives a more distinctly textured effect.

3 When you have finished braiding the hair, apply heat from a hairdryer for speed or leave hair to dry naturally – this will probably take at least 2 hours.

4 When the plaits are dry, remove them and run your hands through the hair to loosen. Style as you like and spray for hold.

Forming a Marcel wave for a retro look

For a retro look use this very old technique, which creates a stylized wave in the hair. It's effective placed throughout the front section to emulate the 'screen sirens' of old. It will take practice to perfect but is well worth the effort.

You will need

- Hairdryer
- Liquid gel or strong-hold styling product
- Comb
- Clips

1 Wash your hair, then blow-dry it to be completely dry.

2 Apply a liquid gel or strong-hold styling product through the top sections of your hair (from the top of your head to ear level), then comb this area smooth.

Stylist's note

For this wave, use flat metal clips, which will hold the hair without leaving an unsightly ridge in the dry hair.

3 Use your fingers to smooth and hold hair from the hairline down, then push the lower hair back up towards the root, creating an 'S'-bend. Hold with a clip.

4 Form a second wave below the first and grip in place. Repeat on the other side. Leave to set, then remove the clips.

Using your fingers to shape shorter hair

You will need

- Comb
- Light styling product

You can achieve fantastic shape and texture in short hair without spending hours in front of the mirror with a hairdryer. The trick is to apply a texturizing product to hair that is just dry, then work the hair into shape with your fingers.

1 Wash your hair and towel-dry it lightly. Comb a light-hold gel, spray or lotion styling product through your hair.

2 Using your fingers, ensure the styling product you choose is evenly distributed though your hair from root to tip.

Stylist's note

Choosing the right styling product for your hair type will help you achieve this look. Ask your salon for advice.

3 Tease the hair into shape using your fingers. Keep lifting it at the roots to add height and to avoid a flat finish.

4 Keep working round your head with your fingers to shape your hair into a style that suits your face and look.

Using gel to create a smooth, wet look on shorter hair

You will need

- Wide-tooth comb
- Wet-look gel

This delightful finish best suits elfin cuts and strong face shapes. It is a great way to accentuate a good head shape and a strong cut. It requires some confidence to wear, but is oh-so-striking. What could be easier?

1 Wash your hair, then towel-dry it to be damp rather than wet. Comb through to detangle using a wide-tooth comb, which won't stretch and break your hair.

2 Squirt some styling gel into the palm of your hand, then rub your hands together.

3 Apply the gel to your hair with your fingers, ensuring it is worked through hair from root to tip and is evenly distributed over your head.

4 Comb your hair into the style of your choice and leave to dry.

Stylist's note

Gel is a product with such great staying power that it can be used to sweep fringes (bangs) to one side and they'll stay put.

Using gel to create spikes on shorter hair

You will need

- Wide-tooth comb
- Gel
- Hairdryer
- Comb

If hair is cut in layers with a mixture of short and long lengths then it is ideal for this look, which makes a striking change from flat or multi-textured short looks. The shorter layers help the longer lengths to stand up more.

1 Wash your hair, then towel-dry it to be damp rather than wet. Comb through to detangle using a wide-tooth comb, which won't stretch and break your hair.

2 Apply gel by tipping the product into the palm of your hand, then working it through the hair, using the fingers to ensure it is distributed from root to tip.

3 Blast-dry your hair with the hairdryer, paying particular attention to the roots to create lift. Direct the airflow to blow from underneath to add volume.

4 Twist random sections of hair, then backcomb these for added height where required and to create defined shape.

Stylist's note

Gel is available in strong, medium and light-hold formulas, so be sure to select one that is right for your hair type.

Using mousse to create a bedhead finish on longer hair

You will need

- Wide-tooth comb
- Volumizing mousse
- Texturizing spray

Work with product to build up texture and volume in your hair, creating a look that is vibrant and youthful. This is a great way to prevent longer hair looking drab or dull and it makes heavier, thicker hair look full of life instead of falling flat.

1 Wash your hair, then towel-dry it to be damp. Comb through to detangle using a wide-tooth comb. Squirt some mousse into the palm of your hand.

2 Rub your hands together, then work the volumizing mousse into your hair from root to tip using your fingers to distribute it evenly.

Stylist's note

When rough-drying hair, run your fingers through the hair frequently to prevent tangles forming.

3 Tip your head upside-down and scrunch your hair up from the lengths to the roots. Leave hair to dry naturally, scrunching your hair again if necessary to add texture.

4 To finish, spritz hair all over with a texturizing spray to enhance the movement and texture you have created.

Fitting and wearing a wig with a natural hair fringe

Blend a wig with your natural hair to disguise problems such as colour regrowth at the roots, conceal ultra-fine hair or to add length. Leaving your fringe free will make the look more natural, but only if you make a good colour match.

You will need

- Comb
- Hairnet (optional)
- Wig
- Hairbrush

1 Comb dry hair to be as smooth and flat as possible. Tuck longer hair into a hairnet to keep it as close and flat to the head as possible.

2 Position the wig on the crown of your head, ready to put on from back to front.

Stylist's note

It's important to place the wig on your head from back to front, keeping your natural fringe lying flat.

3 Draw the wig forward into place, leaving the fringe (bangs) free, and fix the wig in place using the its own inbuilt combs.

4 Style the wig and your natural hair as usual using a hairbrush rather than a comb, as this could pull and displace the wig.

Fitting and wearing a whole-head wig

Ring the changes by wearing a wig! You can alter your hair colour, length and texture in an instant. There is a huge range of wigs available, and modern wigs are light, comfortable and look very natural if they are worn properly.

You will need

- Hairbrush
- Hairspray
- Hairband (headband)
- Hairgrips (bobby pins)
- Hairnet
- Wig

1 Brush dry hair to be smooth and spritz all over with hairspray to keep hair in place.

2 Long hair should be tied up at the back with a hairband (headband). Grip a fringe (bangs) out of the way with hairgrips (bobby pins), to keep the hairline as clean as possible.

3 Place a hairnet over your head to keep hair as flat and as close to the head as possible.

4 Place the wig on to your head, taking care to fit it from front to back and matching up the front edge of the wig base to the front hairline.

5 Pull the back of the wig base down to the base of your head so it's a snug fit.

6 Once the wig is in place it should feel comfortable and match your hairline. Now you can style the hair as usual. Brush smooth.

7 You can apply straightening irons for a sleek finish. You can use heat on man-made fibre as long as you check the manufacturer's instructions first.

8 Finally, spritz your hair all over with medium-hold spray to fix the style in place.

Stylist's note

If you don't have a hairnet to tuck natural hair into, then the foot cut from a nylon stocking will work equally well.

Fitting and wearing a hair weft

You will need

- Hairbrush
- Sectioning clip
- Hair weft

Use clip-in, narrow wefts of false hair as a quick and fun way to jazz up your hair colour. Just pick the colour you want, clip it in and go. When you've had enough, they are simple to remove and can be reused countless times.

1 Brush dry hair to be smooth and tangle-free.

2 Take a section of hair from just below the natural parting and lift it back and out of way (in effect creating a temporary second parting). Secure with a sectioning clip.

Stylist's note

Placing the weft just below the line of your parting makes it easier to disguise the join and blend it in with your hair.

3 Pick up the weft and hold it at the top so that the integral combs face down. Depending on the width of the weft there may be two or more integral combs.

4 Position the weft where you have lifted the hair, then lay the hair back over the weft to conceal the join. Blend the weft with your natural hair.

Fitting and wearing a false fringe

It's so easy to use false hair pieces to quickly change your style. Available with a variety of fixings, from clips to bands and internal grippers, choose between man-made fibre and real hair. Nobody will ever know unless you tell them!

You will need

- Comb
- Light-hold hairspray
- False fringe (bangs) on a band

1 Comb dry hair away from your forehead. Apply light-hold hairspray to smooth the hair further. Select a hairpiece that matches your hair colour as closely as possible.

2 The false fringe (bangs) shown here is on a band to hold it in place. Place the fringe on your forehead and position the band to sit behind your ears, as shown here.

3 Push back the band and draw the fringe up so it sits neatly along your natural hairline. Blend the false hair in with your natural hair.

4 Style all of the hair as usual. You can use heat on man-made fibre as long as you check the manufacturer's instructions first.

Stylist's note

Mixing false and natural hair works best when you are careful to select a great colour match. Ask for a second opinion when choosing as it is easier for someone else to judge.

Fitting and wearing a false ponytail

To lengthen and fill out a natural ponytail so that it becomes fantastically luxurious and more eye-catching, augment your own hair with a ready-made hairpiece. It's an instant solution and can be very quickly and easily fixed in place.

You will need

- Hairbrush
- Hairband (headband)
- Hairspray
- False ponytail
- Hairgrips (bobby pins)
- Shine spray

1 Brush dry hair to be neat and tangle-free.

2 Draw your hair into a ponytail, secure with a hairband (headband) and spritz with hairspray. Use the palms of your hands to run over the sides of your head and calm any flyaway hairs.

3 Position the false ponytail over the natural one. Select a hairpiece that's a good colour match and which is longer than the natural ponytail.

4 This false piece has a crocodile-clip grip mechanism which clasps shut over the base of the natural ponytail.

5 Hide the join by wrapping a small section of natural hair around the base of the ponytail and gripping it in place with hairgrips (bobby pins).

6 Blend the tail of natural and false hair with your fingers.

7 Spritz the ponytail all over with shine spray.

8 You should not be able to see where the false hair is affixed when you have finished; it should look natural.

Stylist's note

When adding a curled hairpiece to straight hair, you will need first to curl your own hair in order to blend the hairpiece more convincingly.

A range of fringe finishes for different effects

A fringe is a great face-framing feature of a haircut that can also draw attention to your eyes and bring out the colour and texture of a hairstyle. It's versatile too. Alter the way you wear a fringe and see how it changes your look.

1

2

3

4

1 Accentuate a strong fringe (bangs) as a feature by blow-drying it smooth and applying a small amount of shine crème. Push the fringe slightly to one side if you like, to soften the look. Super elegant.

2 Eyes peeping out from under a very full fringe can be very seductive. Create this style of fringe by blow-drying it to be ultra-smooth against a textured bob – it's a great dramatic contrast.

3 Opt for a deep fringe on a long style as it keeps the look youthful and fresh. You don't need to wear the fringe all one length – it will be easier to carry off if it is shattered or chopped into slightly.

4 A fringe is a great way to balance a longer, oblong-shaped face and looks great when the rest of the hair is tied back.

5 Moving a parting lower to one side gives the effect of a long fringe worn on one side. Use smoothing crème or spray to keep hair in place.

5

Dressing hair

Once you have mastered the essential skills of drying and setting your hair in various different ways, and adding false hair, you can use this know-how as the basis for dressing your hair in a range of fantastic styles. Over the following pages you will find an array of easy-to-follow step-by-step techniques, from soft finishes, ways to add texture and contrast and fringe (bangs) effects to up-dos, back-dos and pin-ups. You'll be amazed by how much you can do for yourself, so have a go and you'll soon be able to dazzle your friends with your new-found abilities.

Creating a rolling ponytail on mid-length or longer hair

If you don't have the time or enough confidence to put your hair in a full up-do, then this twisted style is perfect as it is easier to do than you think and makes an attractive eye-catching look. Simply roll and go!

You will need

- Wide-tooth comb
- Heat-protective spray
- Sectioning clips
- Hairdryer
- Diffuser attachment
- Hairgrips (bobby pins)

1 Wash your hair, then towel-dry it to be damp rather than wet. Comb through to detangle using a wide-tooth comb, which won't stretch and break your hair.

2 Spritz your hair all over with a heat-protective spray to prevent scorching hair when drying it.

3 Section off the top area using sectioning clips. Position the diffuser under the ends and mid-lengths of your hair and work around your head drying hair in sections, ensuring it rests on the diffuser.

4 Remove the sectioning clips and work through the top section of hair in the same way, until all your hair is completely dry.

5 Take a panel of hair from the front of the ear at one side and start loosely twisting it towards the back of your head.

6 Draw in more hair as you work towards the back of your head, keeping fingers open and continuing to loosely twist the hair.

7 Grip the roll of hair to secure to the back of your head at a point just past the centre.

8 Repeat the process, starting at the other side of your head and gripping this second section over the first at the back. Tease the loose ends to blend and to fan out.

Stylist's note

Diffuse-drying the hair before you create the ponytail adds body and shows off the roll detail of this style to better effect.

Placing ponytails for different effects

You will need

- Hairbrush
- Covered hairband (headband)
- Hairspray

Have you ever wondered how to move on from schoolgirl ponytails to the more sophisticated looks on the fashion pages of magazines or catwalk shows? Perfect placement is the key, so here's the know-how to create a stylish ponytail.

1 Brush dry hair to be smooth and tangle-free.

2 Draw your hair to the back of your head with a hairbrush and grasp with one hand to hold in place.

3 Secure the ponytail with a hairband (headband). A covered hairband rather than an elastic band is best if you have one as it doesn't snag and pull out hair as easily.

4 Here the ponytail is centrally placed with the base at the mid-point at the back of the head.

5 Alternatively, for a low tail, tip your head forward before drawing the hair to back of your head. This will position the base of the tail closer to the nape of your neck.

6 This is how the perfect low ponytail should look. Dress up the ponytail by using a decorative hairband (headband), if you like.

7 For a high ponytail, tip your head backwards before drawing the hair to back of your head. This places the base of the tail higher up the back of the head.

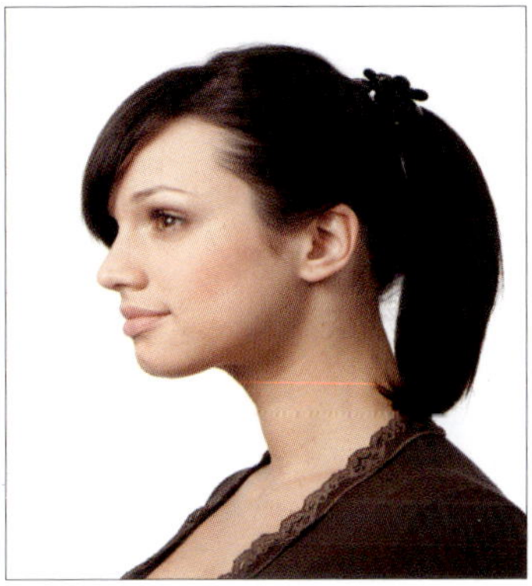

8 This is how the perfect high ponytail should look.

Stylist's note

Take a look at your profile and figure out where best to position a ponytail to complement your head shape.

Creating a perfect plaited ponytail

The technique is simple, but getting a plait to look even and neat is quite an art. Once mastered, you can apply the method in any number of styles. Here is a straightforward plaited ponytail to get you started.

You will need

- Hairbrush
- Covered hairbands (headbands)
- Light-hold hairspray
- Shine spray
- Accessories (optional)

1 Brush dry hair to be tangle-free, then draw your hair into a ponytail at the back of the head, using a covered hairband (headband) to secure it.

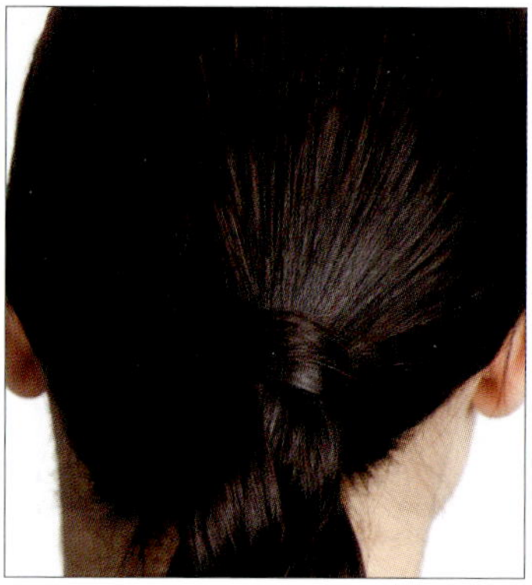

2 Wrap a small section of hair around the hairband at the base of the ponytail for a cleaner finish.

3 Spritz your hair all over with a light-hold hairspray. Don't overdo it or it may make the hair hard to work with – simply spritz spray above the head and allow it to settle on the hair.

4 Divide the loose hair of the ponytail into three even sections.

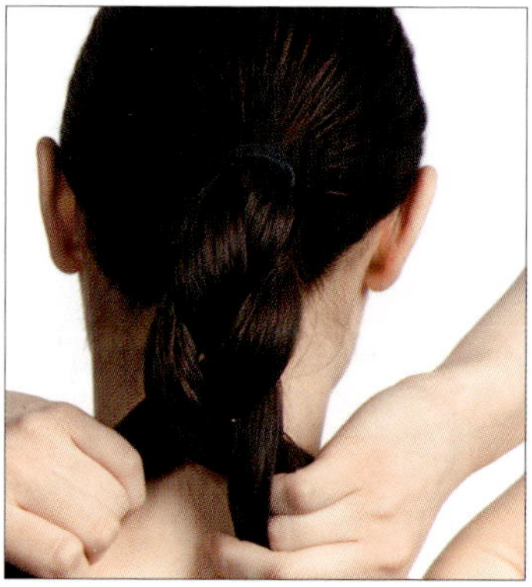

5 Weave the three sections together – taking left over centre, then right over centre and repeating.

6 Continue to weave the hair into a plait (braid) until shortly before the ends of the sections.

7 Secure the ends with a hairband and spray the plait with shine spray.

8 Add accessories to the end of the plait if you like, depending on the occasion.

Stylist's note

Using a light-hold spray before weaving the plait (braid) will calm flyaways and give a neater finish.

Creating a perfect ballerina bun

You will need
- Hairbrush
- Hairband (headband)
- Hairspray
- Hairgrips (bobby pins)

Neat and elegant, the ballerina bun is perfectly suited to a dancer who needs to create beautiful lines and keep hair off her face, and it creates a classic look at other times, too. Once in place, you can accessorize in any number of ways.

1 Brush dry hair to be completely tangle-free and smooth.

2 Draw your hair into a ponytail at the nape of your neck or slightly offset for an individual touch. Secure with a hairband (headband) and spray with hairspray for hold.

3 Take all the free ends of the tail and gently twist them together.

4 Continue twisting more tightly at the back of the head.

5 The tail will start to turn around itself as you continue twisting.

6 Wrap the twisted ends of the tail around the base of the ponytail and grip in place.

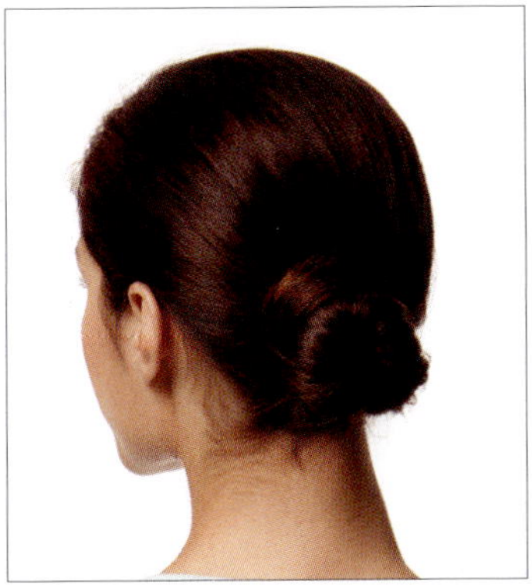

7 The back should look like this when you have finished.

8 Spray with hairspray to hold and to calm flyaway hairs.

Stylist's note

If the look is too severe for your face, then loosen a few tendrils of hair around the face for a softer feel.

Creating a perfect French roll

A chignon by any other name, this is a great up-do that can be dressed to be as chic and sophisticated as you like, or worn looser and casual for a more relaxed vibe. You can add accessories to suit any occasion.

You will need

- Hairbrush
- Wide, open hair pins
- Hairspray
- Accessories (optional)

1 Brush dry hair to be smooth and tangle-free.

2 Draw your hair back into a ponytail with the base slightly to one side of your head at the back, and hold with your hand.

3 Without securing the ponytail with a hairband (headband), twist the hair being held so that it turns round and up to lie flat against the back of your head, forming the roll shape.

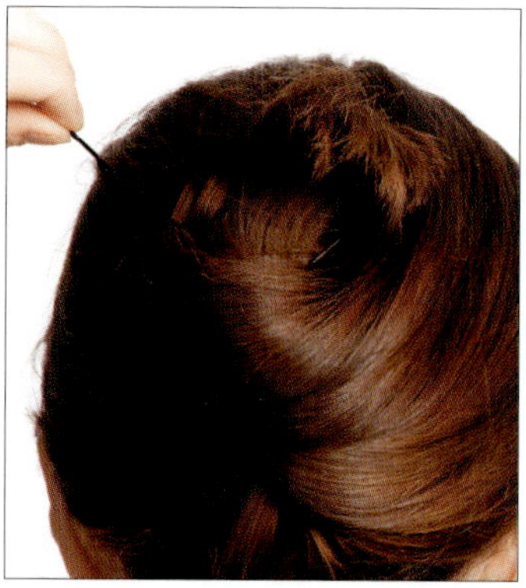

4 Pin the roll in place using open-ended pins, pushing the heads in as far as possible so they don't stick out.

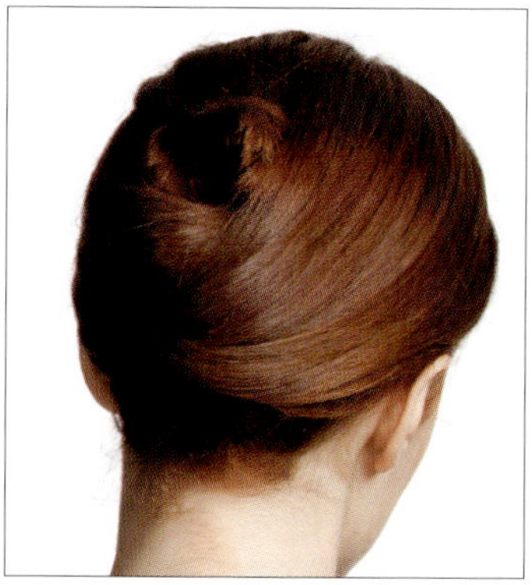

5 The roll should look like this from the back when you have finished pinning the hair.

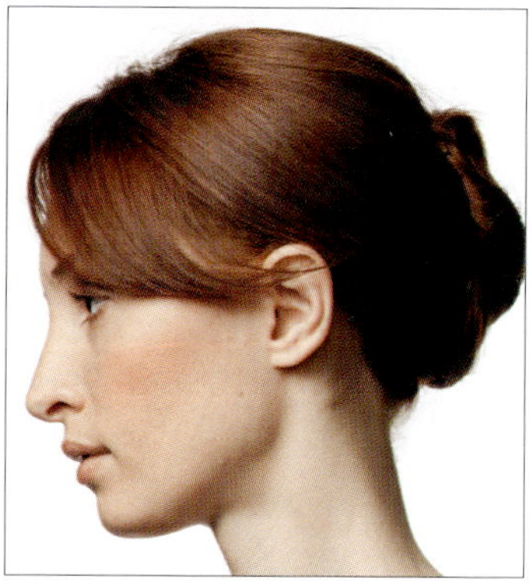

6 The hair should look like this from the side when you have finished pinning the hair.

7 Spritz your hair with hairspray for hold and shine.

8 Add accessories if you like, depending on the occasion.

Stylist's note

Use open pins to secure the hair – as many as you like, provided they are pushed in firmly to conceal them as much as possible.

Creating a perfect woven bun

A simple ballerina bun can look more interesting if you work your hair into a plait first. It's perhaps easier to pin up too, especially when you are working with layered hair, which can be more tricky to style.

You will need

- Covered hairbands (headbands)
- Hairgrips (bobby pins)
- Hairspray

1 Draw your hair into a reasonably tight ponytail at the back of your head, slightly off centre, with an off-centre parting at the front. Secure in place with a covered hairband (headband).

2 Weave the ends of the ponytail into a plait (braid) and secure the ends with a hairband.

3 Wrap the plait around the base of the ponytail.

4 Grip the plait in place to form the bun shape.

5 The smaller end of the plait should sit at the top of the bun as this will accentuate the detail of the weave better.

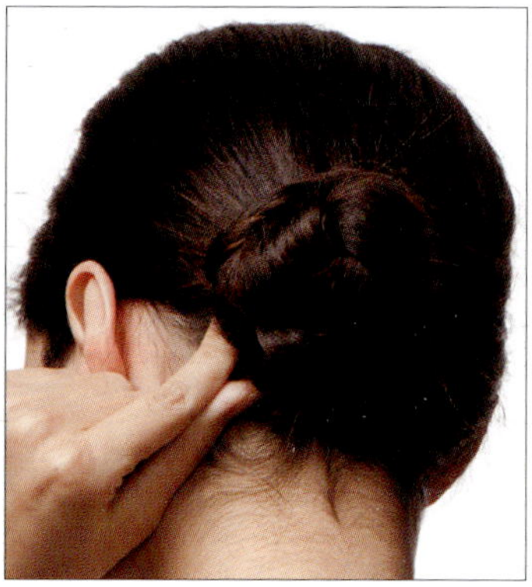

6 Tuck the free ends of the plait into the bun to hide them, and pin in place with hairgrips (bobby pins).

7 This is how the bun should look from the side when you have finished pinning it.

8 Spray with hairspray to hold and to calm flyaway hairs.

Stylist's note

Positioning a bun or ponytail to sit slightly to one side always adds an individual touch.

Creating a perfect French pleat

This is a gorgeous classic look that is particularly good for styling hair that is layered. Once you have mastered the technique, you can choose to pleat hair vertically, off-set or even horizontally for an individual touch.

You will need

- Hairbrush
- Covered hairband (headband)
- Hairspray
- Accessories (optional)

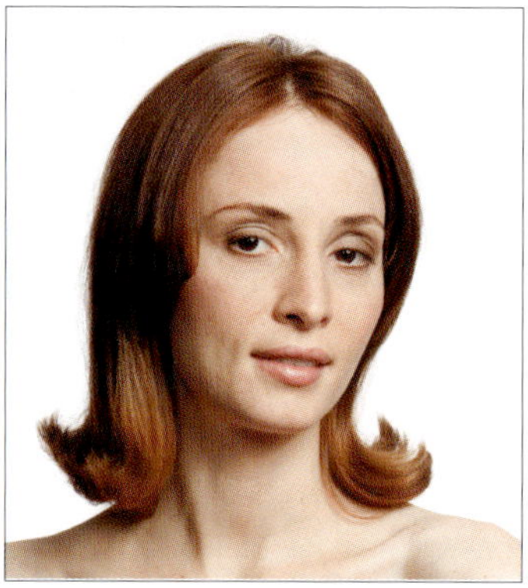

1 Brush dry hair to be tangle-free and completely smooth.

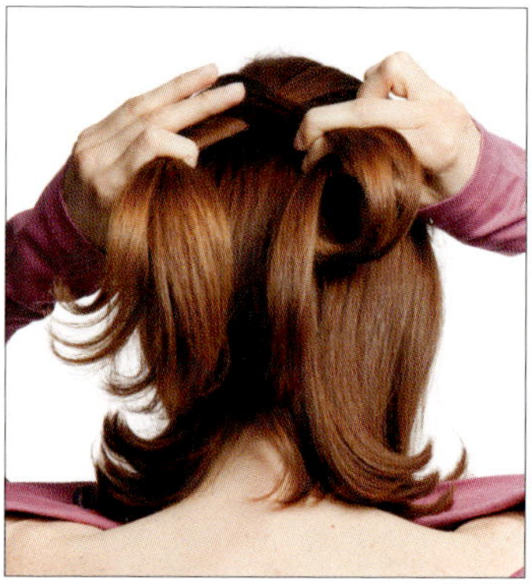

2 Starting at the top of the back of your head, take three even sections of hair from a central point and start to weave a plait (braid).

3 After one or two weaves, draw in small sections of loose hair from the sides as you continue the plait. You should incorporate all the hair from the sides as you go.

4 Secure the plait with a hairband (headband) when you reach the bottom of your hair.

5 Tuck the free ends and any length of plait under the main body of the plait and pin to hold securely.

6 Spritz your hair with hairspray to hold and to keep the look neat.

7 Alternatively, weave a plait from one side of the top area of your head to the opposite bottom side to form an offset French pleat (roll).

8 Add ornamental pins or other hair accessories for effect, if you like.

Stylist's note

The first time you try this style, position a mirror in front of you and one behind so you can see how the pleat (roll) is forming.

Creating a sweet asymmetric back-do

For a dressy style that offers a new and different take on a ponytail, this offset, drawn-back do is perfect. It leaves some hair to nestle around the neck for a softer line, yet is sleek-looking and sophisticated at the same time.

You will need

- Paddle brush
- Hairdryer
- Heated rollers
- Hairband (headband)

1 Brush clean, dry hair to be smooth and tangle-free.

2 Using a paddle brush and a hairdryer work the hair to be as smooth as possible by brushing down the hair as you apply heat.

3 Place heated rollers in the hair but only wind through about three turns (depending on the length of hair) to stop in the mid-length area.

4 Use the rollers' own grips, pins or clasps to hold them in place and allow the rollers to cool completely.

5 Remove all the clips and the rollers from your hair.

6 Lightly brush your hair to loosen but not lose the curl.

7 Part your hair down one side from centre front to the back of your ear. Secure the bigger section in a low ponytail leaving the other section free.

8 Take the loose section of hair and draw it back to go under then round over the base of the ponytail. Pin it in place so it disguises the band and so that all the free ends of hair tumble together.

Stylist's note

This look requires super-smooth hair, so it is important to work in extra smoothness using a hairbrush and a medium-heat setting on a hairdryer, even on dry hair.

Creating a textured twist up-do on longer hair

It's fun to put long hair up into a style that suits both day and night. Rather then smoothing your hair into a really groomed up-do, work with the natural texture of the hair and don't be afraid of leaving ends free for a softer edge to finish.

You will need

- Hairdryer
- Sectioning clips
- Hairgrips (bobby pins)
- Open-ended pins
- Dressing-out brush
- Hairspray

1 Diffuse-dry clean, long hair for added texture and volume. (See pages 116–17.)

2 Section your hair from ear to ear across the top of your head using sectioning clips to form front and back sections, as shown here.

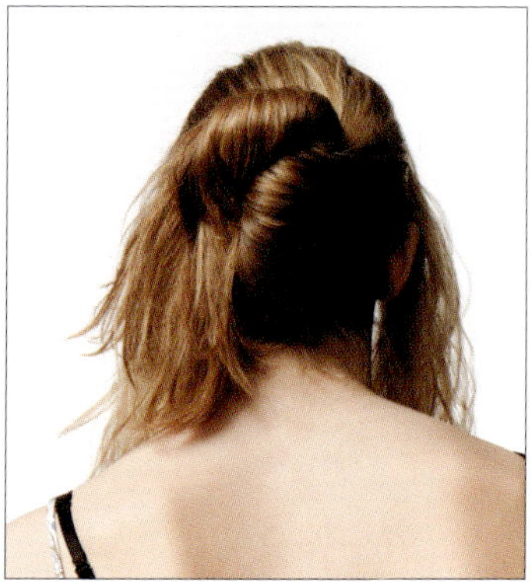

3 Grasp the hair from the back section and twist it up to lie against the back of your head, then turn the ends over to lie as shown. Grip in place with hairgrips (bobby pins).

4 Taking the front section, backbrush the hair near the roots using a dressing-out brush.

5 Continue to backbrush, taking hair from the front hairline and working backwards to the line where the front section finishes.

6 Lift and draw over the whole front section to the back of the head. You should now have a lot of height in the front section.

7 Smooth over the top section using the dressing-out brush.

8 Pin this lifted and backbrushed front section at the back, placing it over the top of the twist created in Step 3. It should look like this. Spray with hairspray to hold.

Stylist's note

You will need to practise this a few times but once mastered, it is quick to do.

Special occasions

For those red-letter days when you really need a hairstyle with 'wow' factor, dress your hair in one of our special occasion dos. Whether you opt for elegance and classic chic or prefer to go for a sophisticated, contemporary style, the art of creating a fantastic look lies in being confident that your style suits you and will stay in place as long as you need it to. Take your time to practise the techniques so that when you come to the big day you will be calm and more than able to finish the hair superbly.

Creating a sleek, elegant finish on shorter hair

A shorter hair cut can be groomed to look just as special as an up-do on longer hair assuming you're prepared to channel effort into meticulous preparation and to select the right finishing products to show off your style.

You will need

- Hairbrush
- Styling lotion
- Large-barrelled curling tongs
- Hairspray
- Shine spray

1 Brush clean, dry hair to be smooth and tangle-free.

2 Put some styling lotion in the palm of one hand, rub your hands together and apply the lotion all over with your fingers, to protect your hair from heat and help to style it.

Stylist's note

If you find you have created too much volume at the sides with the tongs, rescue the look by applying straightening irons from the mid-lengths to the ends on these side sections.

3 Taking sections of hair from the top of your head, place large-barrelled tongs at the ends of the hair and roll up to the roots. This will require one or two turns.

4 When all the hair has been tonged this way, brush through and smooth into shape. Spritz all over with hairspray for hold and shine spray to finish.

Creating a glamorous pin-up on shorter curly hair

You will need

- Hairgrips (bobby pins)
- Hairspray

If you are in need of a great evening look but time isn't on your side, or you don't have much in the way of styling equipment, then curly hair can quickly be pinned into a simple yet effective style that will make you a real belle of the ball.

1 Lift a small section of hair from one side at the front. Draw it back and over towards the opposite side and grip securely in place. Repeat with the other side.

2 Continue to lift and pin hair from one side to the other to build shape and draw hair off your face.

Stylist's note

Grip each new section of hair that is drawn back so that it conceals the hairgrip (bobby pin) inserted to hold the previous piece of hair.

3 Don't clip too much back – you should leave the side area loose as the curls will soften and frame your face.

4 When you have finished clipping, your hair should be drawn off your forehead and show a little bit of height on top. Spritz with light-hold spray to finish the look.

Creating a quick, chic party look on shorter hair

You will need
- Comb
- Styling lotion
- Sectioning clips
- Small-barrelled round brush
- Hairdryer
- Hairspray
- Shine spray

For the times when you have to move quickly from office to party without the luxury of being able to get ready at home, this look is cool yet sophisticated and special enough to wear with any smart evening outfit.

1 Comb dry hair to be tangle-free and to remove any products that may have been applied earlier in the day.

2 Comb through your hair again so it is smooth and spritz all over with styling lotion.

3 Section out the top area of hair. Wrap small sections of hair, one at a time, round a small-barrelled round brush and blast with heat from a hairdryer.

4 When cool, back-comb the hair in the top section at the roots to create height and texture.

5 Smooth back the hair at the sides and spritz with strong-hold hairspray to keep in place.

6 Mould the top section to form a quiff shape and spray to hold, particularly at the roots.

7 Use the palm of your hand to smooth over the hair and accentuate this quiff shape.

8 Spritz your hair again all over with hairspray for hold, and shine spray to finish.

Stylist's note

If the quiff is too long or heavy and won't stay put, then neatly grip it to the top of the head, pushing the hairgrip (bobby pin) in so that as much of it as possible is hidden.

Creating a quick party look on mid-length hair

It's challenging moving straight from work to a special occasion without all your styling tools to hand. Here's a quick look that can be achieved with a travel-sized hairdryer and a round brush and have you looking great in no time.

You will need

- Hairbrush
- Styling lotion
- Round brush
- Hairdryer
- Nozzle attachment
- Sectioning clips
- Shine spray

1 Brush dry hair to be completely tangle-free and smooth.

2 Rub styling lotion into the root area with your fingers to add lift and movement to the hair.

3 Wrap sections of hair around a round brush to create volume and apply heat from a hairdryer.

4 A ceramic round brush works particularly well here.

5 Using sectioning clips, secure each wrap in place while the hair cools.

6 Work around the head, curling and pinning sections of hair but leaving a fringe (bangs) area out, if you have one. Leave for a few minutes to set.

7 Remove the pins, then shake your hair loose and run your fingers through it.

8 Spritz the smoother fringe area with shine spray.

Stylist's note

Use a ceramic round brush, which holds heat (acting as a heated roller) when used with a hairdryer.

Creating a quick party look on curly hair

This look is very fast to put in place and once you know how to do it, you can make it your own by adding individual details such as ornaments. The technique can also be used on straight hair, which you can tong or crimp first for texture.

You will need

- Styling crème
- Smoothing crème
- Hairgrips (bobby pins)
- Open-ended pins
- Light-hold hairspray

1 Start with clean hair that is dry. If you have straighter hair, curl or crimp it for added texture and volume.

2 Apply a smoothing crème with your fingers to define curls and prevent your hair from frizzing.

3 Push all your hair to one side of your head and hold in place with the flat of one hand. Hair at the front should go back and to the side, off your forehead, as shown.

4 With the other hand, secure the hair at the back of the head using hairgrips (bobby pins) criss-crossed in a line down the back of the head.

5 Arrange the hair at the back to fall so it covers these hairgrips. You can do this by twisting the top section of hair and pinning it again with open-ended pins.

6 Using your fingers, loosen the free ends to encourage volume and apply more smoothing crème to define the curl, if necessary.

7 At the front, pull some tendrils of hair free around your face to soften the look.

8 Spritz your hair all over with a light-hold hairspray to finish.

Stylist's note

By criss-crossing hairgrips (bobby pins) you will make the hold more secure.

Creating a perfect wave set

You will need
- Heated rollers
- Hairbrush
- Setting spray
- Serum
- Shine spray
- Light-hold hairspray

Show off a glorious mane of superbly conditioned hair with a stylish set using heated rollers. It's a look that is sexy and alluring if done well. Enhance with finishing products that bring out the natural shine of your hair.

1 Plug in the heated rollers. Brush clean, dry hair with a hairbush to be completely tangle-free, then spritz all over with setting spray, which will help the waves stay in your hair.

2 Starting at the middle top front of your head, take a section of hair in your hand.

3 Wrap this hair around a heated roller and grip in place.

4 Continue to work through your hair from the front to the back and through the sides until all your hair is wound in rollers and gripped in place.

5 Your hair should look like this when you have finished.

6 When the rollers are cool, remove the hairgrips (bobby pins) and take out the rollers.

7 Gently brush through your hair and style how you like.

8 Apply a touch of serum to bring out the curl and spritz all over with shine spray and a light-hold hairspray.

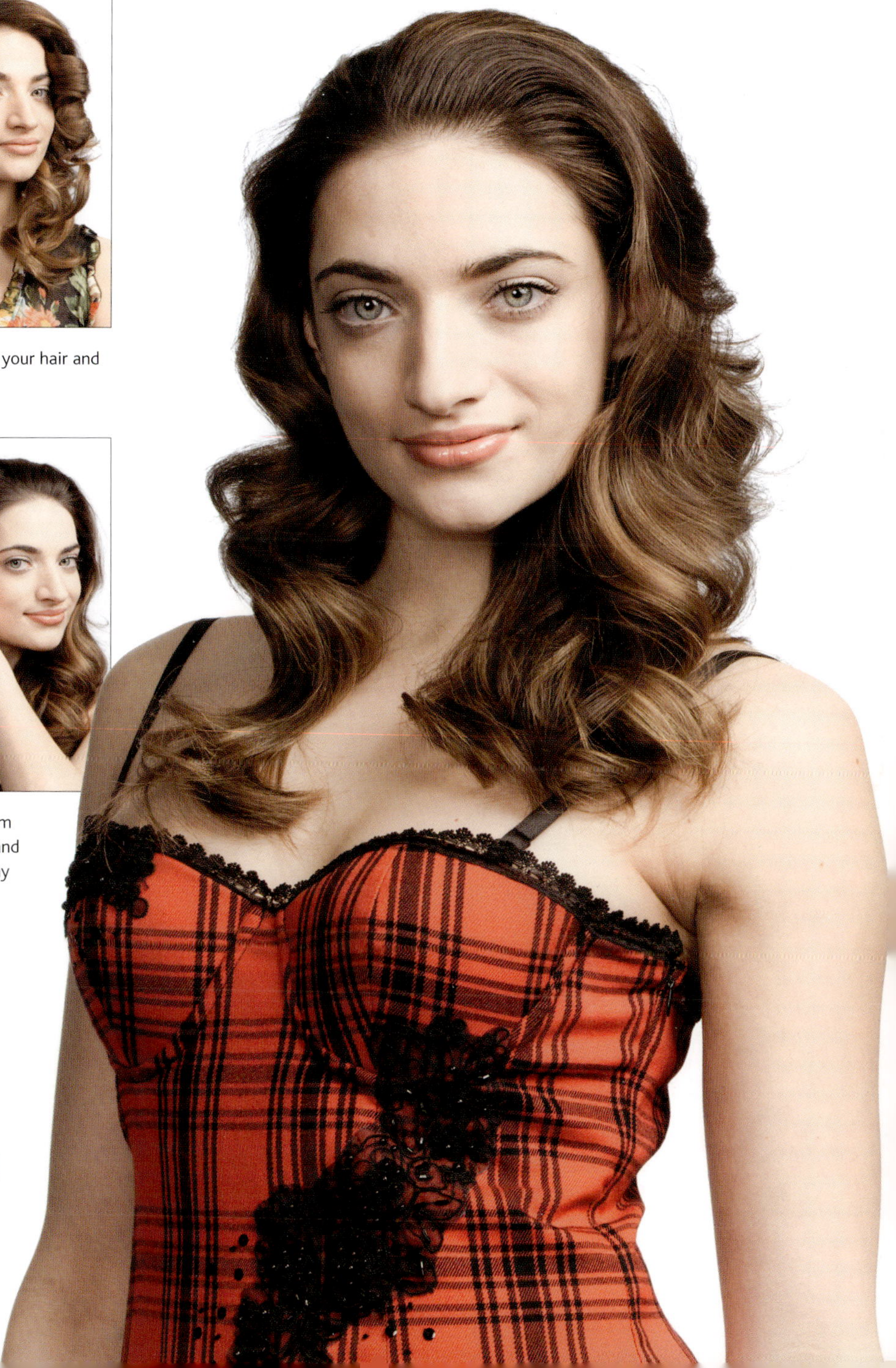

Stylist's note

Work from the top of your head down when putting in the heated rollers – there's no need to section hair first.

Creating sumptuous curls on straight hair

You will need

- Comb
- Heat-protective spray
- Curling tongs
- Pins
- Light-hold hairspray

Transform straight hair into a mass of curls that balance a sophisticated evening dress and look soft and pretty yet grown up and alluring, too. Then simply pin up sections of hair to create a shape and you're fit to go.

1 Comb dry hair to be smooth and spritz with heat-protective spray.

2 Starting at the top front of your head, and working small sections at a time, place curling tongs about one third of the way down the hair. Clamp the tongs shut.

3 Wrap the hair round the barrel of the curling tongs down to the ends of the hair.

4 Work around the head in the same way so that hair is tonged all over.

5 Loosen the curls using your fingers, then tease the hair.

6 Work around your head loosening the curls with your fingers to create a beautiful soft finish.

7 Shape your hair as preferred by pinning up sections.

8 Spritz your hair all over with light-hold hairspray to keep the style neat all night.

Stylist's note

Teasing hair between the fingers breaks up the formality of the curl and makes this a super-soft and pretty finish.

Creating sophisticated ponytails for special events

There are plenty of ways to add interest to a ponytail and keep it fresh on any length hair without the need for ribbons and accessories. Here are few ideas on how to create a really chic finish that looks good from every angle.

You will need

- Hairbrush
- Covered hairband (headband)
- Hairgrips (bobby pins)
- Hairspray
- Shine spray

1 Brush dry hair smooth and draw it into a high ponytail at the back of your head. Secure with a covered hairband (headband), then wrap a piece of hair round the hairband to conceal it.

2 Lift most of the ponytail up and under to form a loop held against the base of the ponytail with your hand. Use the remaining hair to wrap around both the loop and all of the hairband.

3 Pin the loop in place underneath so it is secure and the pins don't show.

4 The ponytail should like this when you have finished.

5 The free ends can be backbrushed to make a fantail and spritzed with hairspray to hold, if you like.

6 Alternatively, make a ponytail low at the base of your neck and positioned slightly off-centre.

7 Roll the tail back under itself and grip in place, leaving one piece of the ponytail free to then wrap round the base and conceal the join.

8 The end can be tucked into the base for a neater finish and pinned in place so it is secure. Spritz with shine spray to finish.

Stylist's note

Always disguise a hairband (headband) by taking a small section of the ponytail and wrapping it round the hairband. Push a hairgrip (bobby pin) through the base to secure it.

Creating a slick offset ballerina bun

For an individual look, put hair up into a classic bun but place it to one side and nearer the front than the back. Accessorize with an ornament or flower and you have a more contemporary take on a traditional style.

You will need

- Hairbrush
- Hairspray
- Covered hairband (headband)
- Hairgrips (bobby pins)
- Shine spray
- Accessory

1 Brush dry hair to be completely smooth and tangle-free.

2 Apply hairspray throughout for added volume and hold.

3 Draw your hair into a reasonably tight ponytail with the base of the tail placed to one side of the front of the head, and secure in place with a covered hairband (headband).

4 Twist the free ends of the ponytail until they wrap back around the base of the ponytail.

5 Grip the twisted bun into place with hairgrips (bobby pins) so it is secure.

6 The bun should now look like this, with the end of the ponytail tucked in neatly.

7 Spritz your hair with hairspray for hold and then shine spray to finish.

8 Add an accessory secured at the base of the bun for effect.

Stylist's note

This style relies on hair being long enough to sweep cleanly round from one side of the head to the other.

Creating a perfect classic chignon

So chic, sophisticated and timeless, a chignon is the perfect up-do for anyone wanting to exude a classic sense of style. You can wear it sleek and groomed or looser and accessorized for a more contemporary feel.

You will need

- Hairbrush
- Comb
- Hairspray
- Hairgrips (bobby pins)
- Open-ended pins
- Fine-waved pins

1 Brush dry hair to be completely tangle-free and smooth.

2 Take an area from the front of the top of your head to the top back and backbrush the roots with a comb to the mid-lengths of the hair.

3 Spritz all the hair that is back-brushed with hairspray to maintain the volume you have created. Draw back this top section and smooth the very top layer with the dressing-out brush.

4 Sweep all the hair at the back horizontally to one side and grip in place with hairgrips (bobby pins) placed in a criss-cross pattern, as shown.

5 Take hold of the loose hair at the back from a point behind the ear. Twist it up to lie against the head. Use open-ended pins to secure along the edge.

6 Take hold of the remaining loose hair from the front side. Twist it loosely and draw it across the back to blend in with the top of the previously pinned twist.

7 Use fine-waved pins to fix this third top section of hair securely in place (fine-waved pins are more easily concealed that standard pins).

8 Tuck in any free ends so they curl inside the top of the chignon roll (use the tail of a comb to ensure all loose ends are tucked out of sight). Spray with hairspray to hold in place.

Stylist's note

You could use a dressing-out brush rather than a comb to create a cloud of angel hair, which adds volume to the chignon shape.

Creating a pin-up on mid-length hair

Pin hair up but leave a strong fringe in place to contrast with the texture at the back and to keep the look more relaxed and softer on the face. You can make the texture at the back as understated or exuberant as you like.

You will need

- Sectioning clips
- Hairbands (headbands)
- Curling tongs
- Hairgrips (bobby pins)
- Comb
- Hairspray

1 Section your hair from ear to ear across the top of the head with sectioning clips. Then section the hair from ear to ear across the back of the head. Centrally part each of the three sections.

2 Secure the middle two back sections as ponytails with hairbands (headbands). Wrap hair round curling tongs to separate each ponytail into three spiral sections.

3 Lift one of the lower back sections to cross over to the opposite ponytail, wrap it around the base of the ponytail, then grip in place. Repeat on the other side. The back should now look like this.

4 Bring each of the upper side sections in turn down to cross at the back of the head then to tuck under the ponytail on the opposite side.

5 Bring the side sections back up to wrap around the base of the ponytail and tuck or grip the loose ends into the base of the ponytail, under the hairband.

6 Back-comb each ponytail to add volume and texture.

7 Fan out the ponytails slightly so the hair covers the gap in the middle at the back of your head.

8 Spritz all of your hair with hairspray to hold.

Stylist's note

Use black, dark brown or blonde hairgrips (bobby pins) according to your hair colour so they are easier to hide.

Creating a twist back-do on mid-length hair

When it seems as though all the special up-dos are best worked on longer hair, here's a great little up-do that works brilliantly with mid-length hair and allows you to leave your fringe free, if you have one.

You will need

- Hairbrush
- Hairband (headband)
- Hairgrips (bobby pins)

1 Brush clean, dry hair with a hairbrush to be completely tangle-free and smooth, then draw it into a reasonably tight ponytail at the back of the head in the middle.

2 Secure the ponytail with a hairband (headband).

Stylist's note

When putting hair up it's best if it's 'day old hair', meaning that is has not been washed for 24 hours. This helps hairgrips (bobby pins) and pins to hold the style.

3 Grasp the free ends of the ponytail and twist to wrap it up round the base.

4 Grip the ponytail at the top and side and don't worry about loose ends and flyaways; it's part of the look.

Creating a twist up-do on longer hair

To contrast with a formal dress, it can be charming to create an up-do that balances an ultra-groomed outfit with a relaxed, softer finish for your hair. This twist up-do is really easy and works well on layered or fine and flyaway hair.

You will need

- Hairbrush
- Open-ended pins
- Hairspray

1 Brush clean, dry hair with a hairbrush to be tangle-free but not super-smooth, then loosely draw it back off the face leaving some hair hanging free at the front.

2 Loosely twist the hair at the back and turn it up so that it lies against the back of the head.

Stylist's note

Once pinned into place, you can continue to pull free tendrils of hair loose until you have the face-framing softness you prefer.

3 Pin the twisted hair into place using open-ended pins.

4 Work some ends into the pinned hair, but leave some hair free for a softer effect. Spritz liberally with hairspray to hold.

Creating a mussed-up back-do on mid-length hair

You will need

- Styling spray
- Curling tongs
- 4 heated rollers
- Hairspray
- Comb
- Hairgrips (bobby pins)
- Hairdryer
- Round brush

Bring out the colours in your hair with a back-do that is fabulously mussed-up and casual from behind yet groomed and styled at the front. It's individual and smart enough for any occasion without looking as though you have tried too hard.

1 Plug in the heated rollers. Spritz dry hair with styling spray. Tong hair through the back using a spiral wind. Wrap the hair at the top of the head in four heated rollers (no more).

2 Remove the rollers when they are cool. Spritz the top section with hairspray at the roots to create lift (tip your head forwards for added volume).

3 Take the top section of hair that was in rollers and gently backcomb the roots to add height. Grip it loosely out of the way at the top of the head.

4 Lift the upper half of the back section, take this hair to one side and grip to hold. Lift the lower half of the back section and grip over to the other side.

5 Your hair should now look like this, with just one piece of hair loose on one side. Spritz with hairspray to hold.

6 Return to the top section and back-comb the ends to create texture, then grip at the back, taking care to conceal hairgrips (bobby pins) as much as possible.

7 You can continue to backcomb and create as much texture as you like, working with the free ends but taking care not to dislodge grips.

8 Blow-dry the fringe (bangs) area round a barrel brush for smoothness and to contrast with the hair at the back

Stylist's note

It makes it easier if you remember you are working with three main sections; top, upper and lower back. Essentially you wrap the back sections across each other and bring the top over to join them.

Creating a glamorous back-do

You will need
- Hairbrush
- Styling spray
- Hairband (headband)
- Open-ended pins
- Hairspray
- Curling tongs

If you want to wear your hair down rather than up, but still be confident of having a style with a 'wow' factor, then this back-do is perfect. It draws hair off the face but still leaves some pieces around the neckline for softness.

1 Brush dry hair and spritz with a styling spray.

2 Section your hair from the occipital area at the back of your head (leaving plenty of hair at the front and nape free) and draw the sectioned area into the centre back.

3 Secure the sectioned hair with a hairband (headband) to form a small ponytail.

4 Draw the hair from one side at the front to cross the top of the base of the ponytail, and hold in place with an open-ended pin.

5 Repeat, drawing the hair from the other side to cross the top of the base of the ponytail, and hold in place with an open-ended pin.

6 This is how your hair should look from the back.

7 Spray with hairspray to hold.

8 Curl any shorter, free front pieces with curling tongs for an individual touch, if you like.

Stylist's note

This is a super-easy style that works well on curly or straight hair of mid- to long-length.

Creating a back-do with extra height

A really glamorous hairstyle needn't be fussy-looking or require you to set your hair first. This back-do is easy to achieve with just some pins and a hairbrush, and it looks fantastically elegant from the front, sides and back!

You will need

- Flat brush
- Hairspray
- Sectioning clips
- Pins or hairbands (headbands)
- Comb
- Hairgrips (bobby pins)

1 Brush clean, dry hair with a hairbrush to be completely tangle-free and smooth.

2 Spritz your hair all over with hairspray to add volume and to help with hold.

3 Section the top area of hair around the crown of your head and pin or tie lower section out of the way with pins or hairbands (headbands). Here, the hair was put in a low ponytail.

4 Working the free top area, back-brush the roots and mid lengths with a comb to create volume.

5 Using a flat brush, smooth over the very top layer of hair and draw it to the back of your head.

6 Undo the lower section that was previously pinned away, and brush through. Grip the hair at the sides for a flatter shape.

7 Your hair should now look like this, with height on the top of your head and smooth sides.

8 Spritz your hair with hairspray for hold and shine.

Stylist's note

Keep checking the side view to ensure you have a sense of height at the top back of your head for an elegant shape.

Creating an elegant top roll up-do

Choosing an up-do that adds height is a great way of appearing a little taller and more statuesque and often prompts you to stand that little bit straighter, too. It's all about conveying poise and elegance to create an impact.

You will need

- Hairbrush
- Sectioning clips
- Hairband (headband)
- Extra-long hairgrips (bobby pins)
- Hairspray

1 Brush dry hair to be completely tangle-free and smooth.

2 Section off the top area of hair and twist and clip it out of the way on top of your head.

3 Draw your remaining hair to the centre back and secure in a reasonably tight ponytail. Wrap a section of hair around the hairband (headband) to conceal it.

4 Your hair should now look like this.

5 Unclip the top section of hair. Brush through then, using your hand to wrap the hair, start to form an upwards roll that adds height.

6 The roll should sit near the top front of your head. Tuck loose ends inside the roll to conceal them.

7 Hold the roll securely in place with extra-long hairgrips (bobby pins) by pushing them inside the roll so they don't show.

8 This is the back view of how the roll should look when you have finished. Spritz with hairspray for hold and shine.

Stylist's note

Once hair is pinned secure and sprayed, resist the temptation to fiddle with the style or keep touching it.

Creating an up-do with a front roll detail

This look is extremely elegant and is a real head-turner for a special occasion. Although it takes some time to do as it requires setting the hair before working the style, it is worth it in order to look and feel a million dollars!

You will need

- Styling lotion
- Hairband (headband)
- Heated rollers
- Comb
- Hairgrips (bobby pins)
- Hairspray

1 Spritz dry hair with styling lotion. Section it from ear to ear over the top of the head. Tie the back section in a ponytail with a hairband (headband).

2 Place a heated roller in the front section of hair.

3 Place a second roller in the front, behind the first one, and one on each side (only use four in total in the front section to create waves rather than overt curl).

4 Place heated rollers in the ends of the ponytail too.

5 Continue in this way until all the hair is wrapped in heated rollers. Allow the rollers to cool completely before removing them.

6 Using a comb, backcomb the front section from roots to mid-lengths. Smooth over the top layer of hair.

7 Wrapping the hair around your hand, roll this front section towards the back of your head and grip in place.

8 Without brushing through, take sections of the ponytail and grip them in loops over the base of the ponytail until they are all gripped in place. Spritz with hairspray to hold.

Stylist's notes

Do practise this style before your big day to build confidence, as it is moderately difficult to create.

Creating a chic, tonged tumbling up-do

You will need

- Sectioning clips
- Hairband
- Small-barrelled curling tongs
- Hairspray
- Bristle brush
- Pins
- Open-ended pins

This fantastic up-do makes a stunning special look that balances a smooth groomed front view with a glorious cascade of hair at the back. It's the perfect complement for a chic evening gown – red carpet hair made easy!

1 Section dry hair to form a front piece, side sections and a back section, which is secured in a high ponytail with a hairband (headband) at the back of the head in the middle.

2 Hang the front section across your face, then wrap small sections of loose hair everywhere else round small-barrelled curling tongs to form ringlets.

3 Spritz hair with hairspray to add volume and guts. Tuck the smooth front piece behind one ear so it is out of the way. Take hair from the top section and backbrush at the roots using a bristle brush.

4 Smooth this backbrushed top section over with a bristle brush and draw it to the back of the head.

5 Wrap this top section hair round the base of the high ponytail to conceal the hairband and pin in place.

6 Lift the free ends of the ponytail with one hand and twist loosely.

7 Wrap the twist round near the base of the ponytail and pin in place, forming a loose bun shape.

8 Pin up all free hair, including the front piece previously tucked behind the ear, around the bun, using open-ended pins to secure, and building up the shape of the bun. Spritz with hairspray to hold.

Stylist's notes

Don't worry about making the back view look too neat. As long as curls are well-defined, pinning them up randomly is fine.

Creating an up-do on curly hair

A mass of natural curls can be a real asset when creating an up-do as you already have movement and texture to build up a fantastic shape. The curls also provide softness around the face and look really adorable.

You will need

- Moisture crème or defining paste
- Hairgrips (bobby pins)
- Hairspray
- Accessory (optional)

1 Allow dry hair to hang naturally without brushing it or trying to smooth it out.

2 Put a small amount of moisture crème or defining paste into the palm of one hand, then rub your hands together and apply it to your hair with your fingers to define your curls.

3 Use hairgrips (bobby pins) to pin up lower sections of hair to create shape and add height.

4 This could now be a finished look for a less dressy occasion.

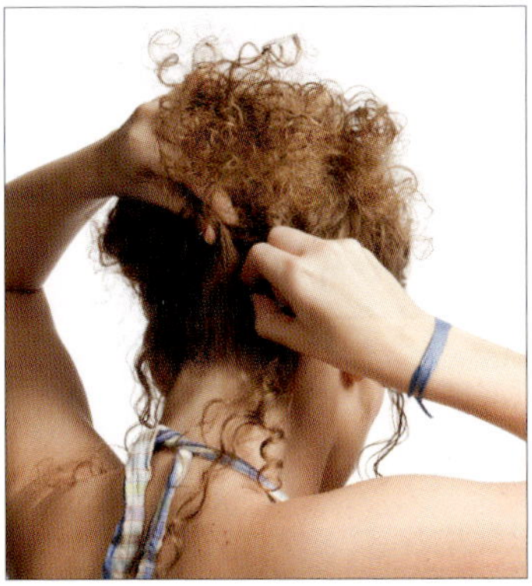

5 Alternatively, continue to pin up more sections of hair for a more dramatic up-do.

6 Loosen small pieces of hair to frame your face and soften the look.

7 Spray your hair liberally with hairspray to hold.

8 Add an accessory to suit the occasion, if you like.

Stylist's note

Sparingly apply a crème or paste to encourage the curls to sit more evenly and retain their natural shape.

Creating an up-do on crimped hair

The crimping detail in this technique adds a really interesting texture to the hair. Also, by crimping hair before you put it up into a style, you will add body so that hairgrips stay put and there is added volume and shape to work with.

You will need

- Sectioning clips
- Hairgrips (bobby pins)
- Wide open-ended pins
- Dressing-out brush or comb
- Hairspray

1 Section crimped, long hair from ear to ear. Working the back section, place hairgrips (bobby pins) criss-crossed just below the occipital bone.

2 Taking all the hair from below the line of crossed hairgrips, roll it outwards from the ends up and pin it in place over the crossed hairgrips using open-ended pins.

3 Lift the hair from the side-front (previously left free) on one side and backcomb the roots with a dressing-out brush or a comb.

4 Wrap this backcombed hair outwards and backwards to form a barrel shape.

5 Grip the wrapped hair behind the ear and tuck in any ends to blend with the back roll formed earlier.

6 Repeat the process of backcombing and rolling on the other side with the remaining loose hair.

7 This is how the back of your head should now look.

8 Spritz your hair all over with hairspray for hold. Don't worry if pieces of hair fly free at the front, it helps to soften the outline

Stylist's notes

This style is stunning but quite complex so ask a friend to help – or position lots of mirrors around you so you can see what you are doing.

Creating a loose wedding style

If you want to wear a tiara or a very striking headdress in your hair, it may be best to wear your hair in a loose style. It's important to place the headpiece far enough forward that it will show clearly in photographs.

You will need

- Heat-protective spray
- Curling tongs or heated rollers
- Strong-hold spray
- Headdress
- Shine spray

1 Create loose curls on your hair by spritzing through clean, dry hair with heat-protective spray then using curling tongs on the hair or setting it on large heated rollers.

2 If necessary, spritz your hair with hairspray for hold, then position the headdress on the very top of your head to sit just behind your ears.

Stylist's note

Always try on a headdress before you buy it to ensure it sits comfortably on your head shape. Check if it's possible to bend it slightly so it fits your head perfectly.

3 Ensure the headdress is not dragging your hair back from the sides; you should be placing the headdress in the hair as it falls naturally, not using it as a headband.

4 Spritz your hair all over with shine spray to finish.

Creating a stylish wedding back-do

For an elegant style that works well with a veil without looking too traditional, then this side-do is perfect. Providing an offset point to fix the veil for a ceremony, it looks equally chic from all angles once the veil is removed.

You will need

- Large heated rollers or curling tongs
- Hairbrush
- Hairgrips (bobby pins)
- Hairspray
- Veil

1 Set your hair in large heated rollers to create loose curls. Brush these lightly and sweep to one side of your head. Twist the hair once and grip in place with hairgrips (bobby pins).

2 This is how the back should look. Spritz the hair with hairspray to hold and calm any flyaway hairs.

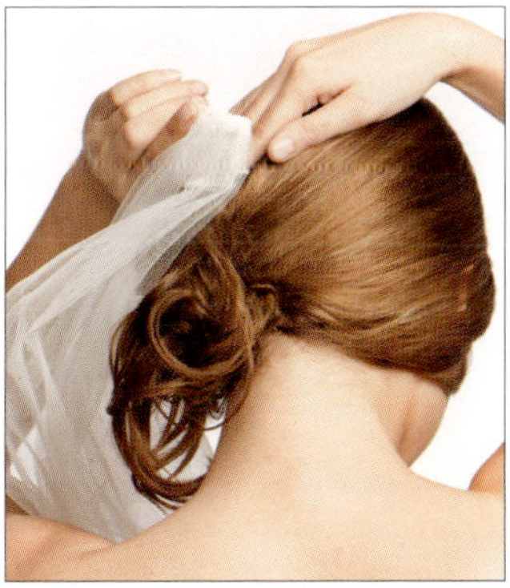

3 Place a veil to grip at base of the twist where there is enough body and texture to secure it properly.

4 This is how the veil will look once it has been positioned correctly.

Stylist's note

Once you have removed the veil, try fixing a new hair ornament in its place, if you like.

Creating a contemporary wedding back-do

For an individual touch, go for an asymmetric look with this side style that works brilliantly with larger or more striking flowers or hair ornaments. It's a fabulous take on a classic technique and will make your wedding day that little bit extra special.

You will need

- Bristle brush
- Hairgrips (bobby pins)
- Flowers or hair ornaments
- Open-ended pins
- Hairspray

1 Brush curled hair to be smooth and tangle-free. Using a bristle brush, gently sweep your hair to one side and hold in place with your hand.

2 Place hairgrips (bobby pins) in a line, as pictured here, to hold the hair in place (use grips to match your hair colour – these are dark for illustrative purposes).

Stylist's note

To create a little bit of height, try backcombing the roots of the top section before smoothing it over and drawing all the hair to the side.

3 Fix flowers or other hair ornaments at the back using open-ended pins to disguise where the hair is already gripped.

4 Spritz your hair liberally with hairspray for hold.

Creating a classic wedding back-do

This look is so effortlessly simple and yet perfect for that fresh, classic feel. It's all about creating a delightful shape that balances and complements the intricate detail of the wedding dress and hair ornament.

You will need

- Curling tongs
- Hair ornament
- Hairgrips (bobby pins)
- Hairspray
- Shine spray

Stylist's note

Choose a hair ornament that is affixed to your hair with a deep comb for added security.

1 Tong clean, dry hair to add waves or very loose curls. The look is natural and romantic without being too over-done.

2 Position the hair ornament (in this case a comb) just below the middle at the back of the head. Check in a mirror that you are happy with its placement and that it is secure.

3 Lift sections from the bottom of your hair and pin them up securely underneath the hair ornament to create shape.

4 Spritz your hair all over with light-hold hair spray to hold, then shine spray to finish.

Creating a romantic wedding pin-up

You will need

- Heat-protective spray
- Curling tongs or heated rollers
- Hairgrips (bobby pins)
- Strong-hold hairspray
- Hair ornaments

Keeping a real romanticism in the hair with plenty of curl detail, this up-do is sweet and beautiful without being too intricate to complete. Place flowers wherever you like at the back – the roses here work well with the softness of the curl.

1 Create loose curls on your hair by spritzing through clean, dry hair with heat-protective spray, then wrapping hair in curling tongs or setting it on large heated rollers.

2 At the back and sides, create an elegant shape by taking random sections of hair and gripping them up. Leave some tendrils free around your face.

Stylist's note

By lifting sections of hair you are aiming to create a clean, strong neckline.

3 Pin the pieces of hair off the neck as this give a stronger line to the look that contrasts well with the loose tendrils at the front.

4 Spritz your hair all over with strong-hold hairspray. Accessorize the up-do with flowers if you like, to complement the dress and romantic mood of the style.

Creating a chic wedding up-do

You will need

- Light-hold hairspray
- Shine spray
- Veil on a comb

For an ultra-sleek line that is superbly elegant and sophisticated, then consider a classic chignon. The simple, clean shape of the hairstyle will help the veil to lie in a lovely cascading fall of fabric and it will also look good once you remove it.

Stylist's note

Wherever you style the chignon to sit will be where you need to fix the veil, so keep an eye on your profile to see which position looks best.

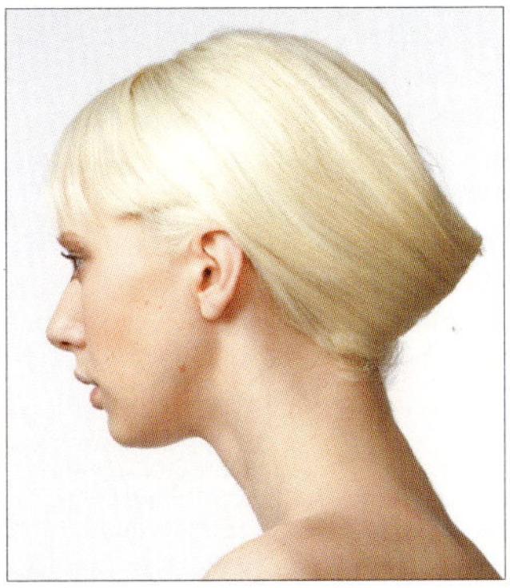

1 Form clean, dry hair into a chignon (see pages 208–9). Spritz with light-hold hairspray and shine spray to finish.

2 Position the top of the veil over the top of the chignon, holding it by the comb, so that the comb attachment is fixed above the coil at the top of the chignon.

3 This is how the top of the chignon should look.

4 Push the comb fixing the veil in place so the veil hangs over the top of the chignon. This is the side view of how it should look.

Wearing a hat

It has been a long time since it was de rigeur for women to wear them, but hats are still a great way of finishing an outfit to look really formal, enormously stylish or simply individual. The trick is in knowing what hat shape suits you and exactly how to wear it.

Apart from grabbing a woolly hat to keep warm in winter, many people only wear a hat on a special occasion and so can feel a bit overwhelmed by the choice on offer. It can be a daunting prospect to find a hat to suit an outfit, event, and hairstyle, but life will be made easier if you figure out several factors in advance:

- Will you be keeping your hat on for much of the time, or do you need a hairstyle that will work once the hat is removed and won't be flattened?
- Does your hat need to be practical in any way – such as providing shade for your eyes, or staying put in inclement weather – or is the hat only ornamental?
- Fix your outfit first, then find a hat, not the other way around. If you feel confident in your clothes, then you'll have more confidence with the hat.
- Remember, you can either wear a hat to complete a look, or you can choose one to be the focal point. The key is not to choose a hat to fight with your outfit – only one will be the winner, the other a sinner!

Proportion and balance

The art of wearing a hat to stunning effect lies in understanding proportion and balance and choosing a size and shape accordingly. A hat can look fabulous on the stand, but that doesn't mean it will necessarily look as good on you, and it's not just a question of how it fits. For example, big hats can swamp petite faces and bodies, or even look like you've got a halo. A small hat might look totally wrong with your hairstyle and maybe even draw attention to your least flattering features.

Equally, the right hat can be worn the wrong way; perhaps too far back, or tilted in an unbecoming way that ruins the overall effect. Here's a simple guide to scale and shape, together with pointers on what works best:

- A large hat will swamp a small face, and if worn with a voluminous outfit, can end up looking rather comical. Instead, wear something that opens up your face, with a small or no brim.
- A cloche or brimless hat can accentuate a round face, and small or close-fitting hats can make a round face look bigger. Choose dynamic shapes and asymmetric lines instead.
- A tall hat on a long face only serves to make you look even more drawn out. Opt for less height and perhaps more width to balance the look.

Above *A hat with width balances a long face shape. Wearing it with some hair or part of the hat coming across the forehead will enhance the shortening effect.*

Above *A round face needs some height and structure to help balance it. Wearing a hat at an angle also serves to vary the line for a more flattering look.*

Above *Wearing a hat (or fascinator) to one side and low over the face is a great way to balance a strong square face shape and is a look that is intriguing and timeless.*

- A wide-brimmed hat on a heart-shaped face can simply make your chin disappear, whereas a hat with an asymmetrical or upswept brim can draw attention to the eyes.
- Rather than try a hat, you can opt for a fascinator (a large ornament), which is ideal for small face shapes or for wearing all day long, from a wedding ceremony to a reception perhaps.

How to wear a hat

A hat is supposed to be worn at an angle to follow the contours of your head; so it works with the outline shape. The result of this is that the hat appears to be a natural extension of your face rather than something that looks like it's following you around and irritating you.

Think of your face and head in four quarters and follow the rules illustrated below. You will first need to decide on your face shape (see pages 36–7).

Tip

When using feathers or ornaments to create a headpiece, the secret is in choosing something with a line that follows the curve of the head. It's much more elegant.

Above *A petite face can be swamped by a large hat, so choose smaller ones and wear them to one side. Details such as veils or ornaments add width for balance and shape.*

How to make and wear a headpiece

If you can't find the exact hat you want, then how about making your own headpiece or fascinator, which does the job without costing a fortune, and works for indoors or out. You can adapt this method to a variety of flowers or other ornaments.

1 Draw hair into a ponytail at the back of the head, fixing it fairly low at the nape and making it as smooth as possible, applying a light gel if required. Calm any flyaways with some hairspray.

2 Take a large fabric flower and bend the wired stem to curve into a half-moon shape that fits the curve of your head. This way it will be more comfortable when it is fixed in place.

3 Use several grips (bobby pins) that fit around the stem to create a way of fixing it to your hair. Try and match these grips to your hair colour to disguise them once they are in place.

4 Place the flower where it best balances your face shape, and complements the outfit. Fix it in place, crossing grips for security, and arrange petals to cover the grips. Spray for hold.

Formal hats

Wearing a striking hat or headpiece usually means you don't need a complicated hairstyle or up-do.

1 An ornate, asymmetric hat worn with a clean, smooth offset ponytail provides dramatic shape that will make a real impact. The point is that this hat works best with a neat hairstyle where hair is swept clear off the face and shoulders for a defined neckline.

2 A large-brimmed picture hat looks fantastic set squarely on the head to contrast with loose, soft hair. It also complements the simple line of the dress. The trick is to wear the hat straight so the brim dips across the forehead slightly.

3 The more decorative the hat, the more you need clean lines in the hairstyle and shape of the clothing; it's important that nothing fights for attention. A hat with height is best avoided if you have a long face. Here, the soft cream is the perfect contrast for a dark hair colouring.

4 A headpiece (sometimes called a fascinator) rather than a hat can be very striking. Here, wearing a headpiece to one side perfectly balances the asymmetric, one-shoulder line of the dress. (It would not work if it were set to the other side of the head, however).

5 The soft feathering detailing of this disc-shaped hat is mirrored beautifully by the soft, gentle curls of the hairstyle and balances the unfussy line of the dress. Having the hat forward on the forehead adds height to a round or square face.

6 A very simple, smooth blow-dried hairstyle is just right for balancing the intricate styling of this dress and the bow detailing of this headpiece. Having a headpiece with the ornamentation to one side adds interest and individuality so the look is not overly demure.

Informal hats

Hats are extremely useful for everyday wear, whether they are used to keep you warm, to shade you from the sun, or simply as a fashion statement. There are many different types and styles, but the same rules regarding proption and balance apply as for formal hats.

1 A peaked cap not only looks good, but has a dual function as it keeps your head warm while shading your eyes from low winter sun. Leave some hair showing to avoid looking too masculine.

2 Woolly hats are perfect for skiing holidays, and help protect your hair from reflected sunlight bouncing off the snow as well as keeping you warm.

3 Sun hats come in many different sizes, so try on several types, from large or floppy to more rigid or structured. It is important they have a brim to offer protection to both skin and eyes.

4 Floppy knitted hats are best worn further back on the head.

1

2

3

4

Choosing accessories

Use hair accessories to instantly enhance a simple hairstyle, or completely change your look. Drawing hair off the face in a hairband or clipping a section of hair to one side with a decorative slide or clip is a neat, fast way to switch styles.

Today's wealth of decorative accessories such as beaded, jewelled, feathered and ribboned headbands, hairbands (headbands), hairgrips (bobby pins) and hair slides (barrettes) mean there is no need to be plain and utilitarian. To help you choose, here are a few top tips:

- Is the accessory to be simply decorative or does it need to hold hair firmly in place? Make sure it will be up to the job.
- It can be a mistake to select accessories in colours that exactly match your clothes, bags or shoes – the overall effect will be a little too cutey pie! Unless that's a look you like, of course.
- For jewelled accessories, less can often be more. If you have high-impact ornaments in your hair, tone down the rest of your jewellery and wear a simple, one-colour top.
- Some accessories, such as headbands and ribbons, are so much associated with schoolgirl looks that you need to be careful to select fabrics and shapes that reflect your personal style today. Velvets, sumptuous satin and grown-up patterns will help.

***Below** Jewelled hairgrips, slides and pins don't need to be large – small ones will still catch the light beautifully.*

***Above** Diamanté clips and slides are very striking, especially in a simple hairstyle, and are best worn with understated jewellery.*

***Above** Flowers have a timeless appeal and there are some really fantastic designs available, from sophisticated to fun.*

- Do experiment at home to be sure you are comfortable before wearing anything adventurous, quirky or particularly dynamic – there's nothing worse than going out and not feeling confident.
- Don't assume accessories are for long hair only. A hair clip or pin in short hair can be fun, glamorous or sophisticated. Just remember that understated can be the best way to start.
- Fast fixes include hair clips or pins placed where there is an interesting detail in the hair to draw attention to, perhaps at the base of a bun or ponytail.
- Tiaras and headbands look good on any length hair but need to be positioned properly: straight across the forehead; high at the base of an up-do; or on long hair in a direct line from ear to ear over the very top of the head.
- Use jewellery to make your own customized accessories. Bracelets can be fixed using hairgrips (bobby pins) pushed through the chain and brooches can be glued on to hair slides or hair clips. You could wrap wire round the ornament and attach to hair slides, hairgrips or combs.
- Newly-washed hair can be too slippery for accessories to stay in. Spritz hair with hairspray to add guts, or even backcomb the roots slightly.
- Remember heavy accessories can drag down or fall out, so don't be too ambitious.

***Left** Work out in advance whether the accessory will need to hold hair in place or whether it is purely decorative, as here.*

Flowers

For special occasions such as weddings, fresh flowers are perfect, but these days there are so many fantastic fabric flowers available that you can look fabulous without fear of your hairpiece wilting.

1 A large flower worn to one side is all the ornamentation this soft, curly hairstyle needs. Place the flower above the ear on the opposite side to where hair is swept (i.e. the same side as a parting).

2 Fabric flowers on bands or gripped to one side of the base of a ponytail are very striking. The longer your hair, the larger the flower should be to prevent it looking too indistinct.

3 Place a flower at the base of a bun for a simple, effective detail. Having the flower to one side or slightly below the top of the bun is more elegant than placing it above the bun.

4 An exaggerated flower adds drama to a ponytail. The larger and more ornate the flower, the more clean and sleek the hairstyle and clothing need to be.

1

2

3

4

Hairgrips and hair slides

Ornamental hairgrips, hair clips, hair pins and hair slides can be a subtle way to draw the eye to a detail in the hairstyle, without being too high impact. Choose a colour that complements your hair tone and your outfit.

1 Two matching hair slides (barrettes) can be pinned to the swirl detail of a simple up-do to lend it an elegant touch for a special occasion.

2 Here a pair of elegant shell-shaped pins contrast with the curl in the hair and emphasize the twist.

3 Highly decorative hair slides add glamour to a pretty hair style, and are especially useful for weddings or other special occasions.

4 Even small, pretty hairgrips (bobby pins) can make a statement. Here, the subtle sparkle finishes the style perfectly.

1

2

3

4

Bows and ribbons

There is a wide range of bows on offer, from tailored to floppy, and they often come ready-tied and attached to hair clips or hair slides. You could also simply form them yourself from ribbons or fabric that matches or contrasts with your outfit.

1 Most ribbons, especially those made from silk or satin fabric, will be too slippery to hold hair in place, so wrap them over a hairband (headband).

2 Adding a neat, ready-made bow lifts a simple ponytail in an understated way. It is smart enough for most formal occasions or can be worn for a night out.

3 Try winding a ribbon round a long section of hair and finishing with a loose bow for a different look.

4 Decorative bows can be attached to hair slides (barrettes) or hair clips, and add interest to a simple, neat style.

1

2

3

4

Scarves

Use a scarf to keep hair tidy, add a certain flair to an outfit, or even disguise unkempt hair. There are so many ways to tie scarves, ranging from turban-style covering the whole head, as a hairband, or as a wrap for a bun or ponytail.

1 Use a small, square scarf to decorate a ponytail or bun. Fold the scarf in half to form a triangle, then place it over the bun with the ends wrapped around the base, then passed back over the top and tied.

2 Wearing a scarf bandana-style covering the top of the head is an alternative to wearing a hat and offers some protection from sun and wind.

3 Use a long, but lightweight, scarf to wrap loosely over your head and shoulders but always leave some hair visible to soften the look.

4 Scarves that cover the whole head are an integral part of many cultures, and are available in a huge range of colours and patterns.

1

2

3

4

Tie a headscarf

Long or mid-length hair can be effectively kept off the face by using a long scarf. Here's how to fix them properly:

1 Hair should be loose and tangle-free with a parting placed where you want hair to fall.

2 Place a long scarf around the head to sit over or just behind each ear, and use the same knot as you would for a necktie.

3 The finished knot can be as exaggerated or as tight as you like.

Stylist's note

A scarf in a slippery fabric may need to be gripped behind the ears to help keep it in place.

Headbands

So easy to wear yet not so easy to pull off in many respects, a headband worn the wrong way looks childish and unflattering. For long or short hair, pulling a headband up over your face to sit on your head passing over or just behind the ears is the neatest way to draw hair off the face, but be careful as it is an uncompromising look. Ensure there is hair visible from the front either at the crown – in the Sixties, backcombing the roots to create height was popular – or leave loose hair at the sides to frame the face. Or, leave out some hair from the fringe for a more casual look that is kinder and less exposing.

1 A wide headband can be worn low on the forehead but with long hair flowing softly to frame the face for a gentler line. This look is ideal for casual daywear, or for keeping hair off your face on the beach or when travelling.

2 A clean-looking narrow headband can add the finishing touch to a smart, formal hairstyle, drawing attention to the up-do in an understated way that doesn't compete with a special dress. Earrings should also be subtle.

3 Adding formality to a very casual up-do, a simple headband in a luxe velvet, silk or satin fabric can be an effective way to upgrade the look. It's quick and easy, too. Selecting a headband in a neutral shade so that it doesn't compete with big jewellery means that the look retains an air of artful charm.

1

2

3

Glossary of terms

There is a wide range of tools and techniques used in hair styling, many of which are described in detail in the front section of the book. In addition, there are some more specific or unusual terms, some of which are listed here:

Anagen phase
The first phase of hair growth, when hair actively grows. It lasts between 2–6 years.

Blow-drying
Hair can be dried using a hairdryer to achieve a range of effects, from a smooth finish to added volume and texture.

Blow-dry lotions/styling crèmes and sprays
A single-application product, these add guts and hold while blow-drying and help protect the hair.

Blunt cutting
When the ends of hair are cut straight across with scissors.

Braids
These are fine plaits (braids) made from small sections of hair, which hang away from the head, unlike cornrows, which are plaited so they sit on the scalp.

Brushes
Used primarily for detangling and smoothing hair as well as shaping a style, there is a number of different types for different uses, including: flat or half-round brushes; paddle brushes; pneumatic brushes; vent brushes; circular or radial brushes and dressing-out brushes.

Catagen/transitional phase
The second phase of hair growth, when hair stops growing but activity in the dermal papilla continues. It lasts between 3–4 months.

Chemical processing
A service to be carried out by a professional salon hairdresser, this refers to any technique that uses chemicals to alter the structure of hair, including perming and straightening.

Chemical relaxing
Especially used to straighten Afro hair, relaxants change the structure of hair to straighten it permanently. This should be done at a salon.

Clips
Used for holding hair out of the way during styling or to pin hair back, clips are available in many different shapes, sizes, colours and patterns. Some may have ornaments affixed to them.

Combs
An invaluable tool for styling hair, combs are available as wide-, medium- or narrow-toothed varieties or as Afro combs, for curly hair.

Combination hair
A common type of hair, this is defined as being oily at the roots, but dry and sometimes split at the ends.

Conditioners
As with shampoos, there are many different types of conditioner available. Choose one that is suitable for your hair type. Some are for everyday use, while others have a more intensive effect or can treat problems, such as dry or damaged hair.

Cortex
This is the middle layer of a hair, under the cuticle and surrounding the central medulla. It comprises fibre-like cells that give hair its strength and contains the pigment melanin, which gives hair its colour.

Cowlick
This effect occurs when hair on the front hairline grows in a swirl backwards, then forwards.

Crown
The highest point of the head, towards the back of the skull.

Crimping irons
These electronic irons are used to add wave-like crimps to hair, which is clamped between the blades and held briefly in place to set.

Curl activators
These products encourage bounce and movement in naturally curly hair.

Curling tongs
This electrical tool is used to wave or curl hair, which is wrapped around the hot rod, clamped in place and held for a few seconds.

Curly hair
Naturally curly hair occurs when the distribution of keratin cells around the dermal papilla is uneven, which causes the hair to grow at an angle. Keratin cells occuring on alternate sides on the shaft cause the hair to grow first one way then the other.

Cuticle
The outer layer of a hair, the cuticle comprises overlapping scales that form a protective shield.

Demi-permanent colour
This treatment is a way of adding, rather than changing, hair colour and will last up to 20 washes.

Dermal papilla
The living part of a hair that is below the scalp in a depression called a follicle.

Dermis
The scientific name for skin.

Double crown
When there are two pivots of natural hair at the top of the head instead of one.

Dreadlocks
The result of twisting and locking together hair into sections, dreadlocks are permanent.

Dressing hair
The art of folding, tying or wrapping hair into different shapes and designs. This is a temporary effect that does not involve cutting, setting or chemical processing, and can be brushed or washed out.

Dry hair
This type of hair looks dull, tangles easily and feels dry. It is caused by a lack of moisture in the hair.

Face shapes
An important factor to consider when choosing a style and cut as well as a hat, face shapes can be: round, oval, square, heart-shaped or oblong.

Fascinator
A large ornament that can be worn in hair in place of a hat, fascinators are often highly decorative and can be made from flowers or feathers.

Forehead
This is the part of the face between the hairline and the eyebrows.

Gels
Used for precise styling, gels can be used to mould or tame hair, reduce static and frizziness, define and shape curls, heat set and more. Wet gel can be used to create a slick effect when it dries.

Graduation
This type of common cut involves creating top layers that are shorter than the ones underneath.

Greasy-looking hair
This type of hair is often lank and oily due to overproduction of sebum. It is often associated with adolescence or hormonal changes.

Grey or white hair
Usually associated with ageing, this type of hair is the result of a lack of melanin granules in the cortex. Grey or white hair tends to be coarser than younger hair and can absorb pollution or chemicals more easily.

Hairline
The line where the hair growth starts on the head and neck.

Hair colour
Natural hair colour is determined by the combination of melanin granules that occur in the cortex.

Hairdryers
Extremely useful for drying and setting hair, there is a huge range of hairdryers available, each with different features and modern technologies. Handbag- or travel-size ones are also available, although they may not be very powerful.

Hair shaft
The visible part of a hair that comes out above the skin.

Hair texture
Race, natural colour and the diameter of each hair determine the texture of hair, which may be fine, medium or coarse. Many people have a combination of different textures.

Hairspray
Used to finish a style, hairsprays fix a style in place and calm flyaways. They can also be used to add guts when back-combing hair.

Heat-protective sprays
This will help protect hair from damage caused by heat or heat-styling tools.

Hair type
The natural condition of hair – its dryness, softness or oiliness. Hair can be normal, dry, greasy, combination or white or grey.

Highlights
These are lighter strands of hair that are achieved by bleaching sections of hair at a salon using foils or a cap.

Hot brushes
Used for lifting roots and adding curl or wave, hot brushes are electronic devices with ceramic barrels that grip hair as it is wrapped around the brush. They are left briefly in place, then removed.

Hot sticks
Similar to rods or shapers, hot sticks are preheated before being applied to hair and left to cool. They add wave or curl to hair.

Keratin
The protein that is responsible for the make-up of hair.

Layers
This is when horizontal sections of hair are cut to the same length around the head. They can be any length.

Lowlights
These are darker strands of hair that are achieved by colouring sections of hair at a salon or at home.

Medulla
The core of a hair, comprised of keratin interspersed with spaces.

Melanin
A pigment contained in the cortex, which gives hair its colour.

Mousse
Designed to give hold, smooth frizz and lift roots, mousses are infinitely versatile and can be applied to dry or wet hair.

Nape
This is the lowest point of the head, where the neck and head meet.

Normal hair
This type of hair is defined as neither greasy nor dry and has been left in its natural state.

Occipital bone
The point on the back of the skull that sticks out the furthest.

One-length bob
Also called a pageboy, this is where hair falls to the same length all round the head, usually sitting on the shoulders or above.

One-length cut
Where hair falls to one length, no matter how long or short, it is called a one-length cut.

Permanent colour
This refers to a permanent colour change caused by a chemical treatment that will not wash out.

Perming
This refers to the permanent techniques that add varying degrees of wave or curl to hair. There are different ways of achieving results, including acid, alkaline and exothermic perms. Among the different results are: body perms; root perms; pin curl perms; stack perms; spiral perms and weave perms.

pH
This refers to the acid/alkaline level of a substance, and is calculated on a scale of 1–14. Shampoos have different pH levels, depending on what they are used for.

Pins
Often used for securing up-dos and back-dos or taming wayward hair, pins are very versatile and easy to conceal in the hair. There are several different types, which provide varying levels of grip.

Point cutting
A way of cutting with scissors pointed into hair to break up any straight lines.

Razor cutting
Using a razor instead of scissors to create movement and softness and taper hair.

Restructurants
Used to repair and strengthen hair, restructurants penetrate the cortex and are especially useful for damaged hair.

Rods or shapers
These are bendable tubes around which hair is wrapped and left to set.

Rollers
Used to add curl or wave to hair, rollers can be clipped in place and heat applied to set the effect, or there are self-heating types that do not require additional heat.

Round-layered cut
Also called a French crop, this is a basic, rounded, layered shape.

Scalp
The skin covering the surface of the head.

Sebaceous glands
Present in the dermis, these glands are linked to hair follicles and release sebum.

Sebum
An oil composed of waxes and fats, sebum acts as protective coating to the entire hair shaft and gives hair its shine.

Semi-permanent colour
A way of adding, enriching or darkening colour, it usually lasts for 12–20 washes.

Serums/glossers/polishers/ shine sprays
All of these products improve the shine and softness of hair, combating frizz and static and improving the appearance of split ends.

Setting
The word for using heat to temporarily set waves, curls or crimps into hair or to straighten hair.

Shampoos
Although there are many different products available, all shampoos are designed to clean your hair and wash away grease and dirt. Some formulations will tackle common problems, such as dandruff or oily hair. Chelating or clarifying shampoos help remove mineral deposits or a build-up of products from hair.

Shattered cut
This is when hair is cut so it has wispy or jagged ends, adding volume and softness to the style.

Skin test
The application of a dab of hair dye to a discreet patch of skin at least 48 hours before hair is coloured.

Slide cutting
Used to remove bulk without affecting the line of a cut, this gives a soft finish.

Snagging
The action of pulling out hairs during combing. This should be avoided, as it thins hair and causes it to break.

Square-layered cut
Sometimes called box or graduated layers, this cut combines layering and graduation. If hair is blown back off the face it forms a square shape.

Straight hair
This occurs when the distribution of keratin cells around the dermal papilla and the hair shaft is even.

Temporary hair
From full-head wigs and clip-on ponytails to false fringes (bangs), wigs without fringes and coloured wefts, there is a wide range of temporary hair on offer.

Thinning
Removing bulk from hair using scissors or a razor.

Volumizers/thickeners
Applied to damp hair before styling, these products are designed to plump up fine or lifeless hair.

Waxes/pomades/creams
Designed to add definition and hold, these are used for creating up-dos and controlling frizz.

Widow's peak
A descending, V-shaped point on the hairline, usually above the forehead.

Acknowledgements

Thank you to Goldwell & KMS California for supplying styling products and arranging their partner hairdressers and for the use of The Goldwell Academy in Mayfair. Particular thanks for help and support to:

- William Wilson – Head of Creative Direction (Goldwell & KMS)
- Sarah Clohessy – Marketing Director (Goldwell & KMS)
- Samantha Field – PR & Marketing (Goldwell & KMS)

The Publisher and Nicky Pope would also like to thank the following for their hard work during the photoshoots or for supplying equipment:

Hairdressing team

- Mo Nabbach at M&M Hair Academy, London
- Margaret Nabbach at M&M Hair Academy, London
- Rachel Hurley, Educator at The Goldwell Academy, London
- Kelly Stone at Elements, Bishops Stortford
- Michael Barnes at Michael Barnes Hairdressing, Covent Garden
- Amanda Brooke at Hair Associates, Taunton
- Claire Cole at Hair Associates, Kingston-upon-Thames
- Angie Mitchell at Desmond Murray Hairdressing, Covent Garden
- Ross Dilanda at Scully Scully, Godalming

Styling

- Clothes supplied and models dressed by Bernard Connolly, clothes stylist

Make-up

- Tracey Wilmot
- Liz Arimoro
- Linda Andersson

Hair appliances and tools

- All hair appliances and some tools and equipment supplied by BaByliss Pro (www.babyliss.co.uk)

Accessories

- Hair extensions by American Dream (www.americandreamextensions.com)
- Hair ornaments and accessories supplied by Johnny Loves Rosie (www.johnnylovesrosie.co.uk)

Hats and headpieces

- Philip Somerville
- Philip Treacy
- Chanel
- Dior

Picture Credits

All pictures © Anness Publishing Ltd, apart from the following:
t = top; b = bottom; r = right; l = left; c = centre

Babyliss 31bc, 96, 97, 98bc, 99tl, 100, 101.
Balmain Extensions (Hair by Steven Goldsworthy, Balmain Global Ambassador and Jason Smith, Artistic Director; photography by Jim Crone; make-up by Lucy Pook; styling by Bernard Connolly.) 75 (4), 76 (9), 86 (8, 9, 10 & 11), 87 (14, 15, 16 & 17).
Corbis 11tl (Visuals Unlimited/Corbis), 11tr (Visuals Unlimited/Corbis), 24bl (Jerome Tisne/Corbis), 97tl (Rick Gomez/Corbis).
Cyndy Hay (Hair by Cyndy Hay, Haze@ no. 10; photography by James Rudland; make-up by Mel.) 58 (20 & 21), 85 (7).
Hatstand Nelly (Hair by Lorraine Watson and Jan Lippe; photography by Jim Crone; make-up by Lucy Pook; styling by Bernard Connolly; hair extensions supplied by Balmain.) 58 (22), 61 (33), 63 (39).
Headquarters (Hair by Headquarters artistic team; photography by Jim Crone; make-up by Lucy Pook; styling by Bernard Connolly.) 59 (23), 62 (37).
iStockphoto 6 (Quavondo Nguyen), 9bl & 15tr (Stephanie Swartz), 9bc & 22bl (Viorika Prikhodko), 9br & 27b (Alexey Tkachenko), 12bl (Jaroslaw Wojcik), 12br (Luca di Filippo), 13 (Andrea Laurita), 14bl, 14tr, 14br (Vasiliki Varvaki), 15tl (K. Govorushchenko), 15tc (Elke Dennis), 16bl (Ross Elmi), 16bc (Jacob Wackerhausen), 17tl (Diane Diederich), 18bc (Dragan Trifunovic), 19bl (Ana Abejon), 19tr (Christine Glade), 20bc (Michael Courtney), 20br (Jim Jurica), 21tc, 23tl, 24br, 26bl (Georgina Palmer), 26tr (Paul Cowan), 28tr (Zsolt Biczó), 28br (Ron Hohenhaus), 29br (Quavondo

Nguyen), 30 (Andrey Yakovlev), 31tl (Graça Victoria), 31tr (Tommy Ingberg), 33bl & 42 (Hadrian Kubasiewicz), 33bc & 38 (Matjaz Boncina), 33br & 48 (Ira Bachinskaya), 34t (Chris Bernard), 35 (Jacom Stephens), 36t (Rudolf Kotulán), 37t, 38 (Matjaz Boncina), 39tc (Eliza Snow), 39tr (Andrea Gingerich), 41tl (Ivan Mateev), 41tr (Anna Bryukhanova), 41cr, 43t, 43bl (Josh Webb), 43br (Christine Glade), 44 (Jacob Wackerhausen), 45tl (Martina Ebel), 45tr (Santino Ambrogio), 45br, 46 (Izabela Habur), 47tl (Gunther Beck), 47tr (Phil Date), 48tl (Ira Bachinskaya), 48tr (G. Powers), 49bl (S. Robertson), 49tr (Snyder), 50bl, 50br, 51tr (R. Elmi), 51bc (F. Romero), 51br, 62 (36) (K. Govorushchenko), 64 (2) (Q. Nguyen), 65 (4) (O. Ekaterincheva), 65 (6) (E. Ogan), 68 (19) (Q. Nguyen), 68 (20, 21 & 22) (K. Govorushchenko), 69 (22) (D. Tulchevska), 69 (23) (K. Kruse), 68 (19) (Q. Nguyen), 68 (20, 21 & 22) (K. Govorushchenko), 69 (22) (D. Tulchevska), 69 (23) (K. Kruse), 69 (24) (Q. Nguyen), 69 (25) (K. Kruse), 70 (26, 27, 28, 29, 30 & 31) (K. Govorushchenko), 71 (32) (L. Banks), 71 (33) (F. Camhi), 71 (34) (S. Starus), 71 (35) (J. Horrocks), 73 (37) (J. C. Justice Jr.), 73 (38) (L. Dodz), 73 (40), 75 (3) (K. Govorushchenko), 77 (12) (M. Honeycutt), 77 (13) (N. Vaclavova), 77 (16) (Q. Nguyen), 77 (17) (K. Govorushchenko), 78 (19) (J. Trenchard), 78 (20) (I. Kurhan), 79 (22) (K. Govorushchenko), 79 (23) (D. Pepin), 79 (24) (F. Backx), 79 (25) (K. Govorushchenko), 80 (26) (A. Ozerova), 80 (27 & 28) (K. Govorushchenko), 80 (29) (V. Casarsa), 82 (35 & 39) (Q. Nguyen), 82 (36) (V. Vitaly), 82 (38) (R. Christensen), 83 (40) (Q. Nguyen), 88 (18) (K. Govorushchenko), 88 (19) (M. Rzymanek) 88 (20) (F. Backx), 91 (29 & 30) (L. Dodz), 92 (31), 93 (35 & 38) (K. Govorushchenko), 93 (36) (P. Piebinga), 93 (37) (T. Marvin), 93 (40) (Q. Nguyen), 93 (38) (F. Backx), 96 tr (S. Hogge), 98bl (N. Siverina), 98br (C. Baldini), 98tc (A. Balcazar), 98tr, 99tc (V. Anyakin), 99bl (L. Gagne), 99br (E. Bonzami), 102, 103t (K. Deprey), 103b, 104bl, 104tr, 105 (L. Williams), 238 (1), 238 (2) (S. Radosavljevic), 238 (3) (P. Han), 238 (4) (P. Hakimata), 240bl, 240bc (T. England), 240tc (J. Fontanella), 240tcr (M. Baysan), 243 (2) (A. Bryukhanova), 244 (2) (K. Govorushchenko), 244 (3), 244 (4) (P. Hakimata), 245 (1) (S. Radosavljevic), 245 (2) (J. Horrocks), 245 (3) (K. Govorushchenko).

Jo Hansford Collection
57 (14), 61 (30), 67 (13), 69 (24), 77 (15), 76 (10 & 11).

Johnny Loves Rosie 240ct, 240tr.

Karine Jackson (Hair by Karine Jackson; photography by Andrew O'Toole; make-up by Margaret Aston; styling by Emma Cotterill.) 55 (8), 62 (34), 75 (7), 85 (2 & 6), 87 (12 & 13), 88 (20).

KJM Salons (Hair by Kerry Mather and the creative team at KJM Salons; photography by Jim Crone; make-up by Valerie Ferreria and Lucy Pook; styling by Cora Chung and Bernard Connolly; hair extensions supplied by Balmain.) 54 (2), 55 (3 & 5), 57 (18), 65 (5), 85 (5).

Michael Barnes (Hair by Michael Barnes for The Goldwell Academy; photography by Kyoko Homma; make-up by Sabrina Ziomi.) 55 (4), 58 (19), 61 (31), 62 (35), 66 (9), 75 (6), 76 (8), 81 (30, 32 & 33).

Pat Wood for Affinage (Hair by Pat Wood for Affinage; photography by David Howard; make-up by Nora Nona; styling by Robie Spencer.) 53 (right), 57 (17), 64 (1), 67 (16), 89 (21, 22 & 23).

Rae Palmer (Hair by Rae Palmer for Rae Palmer Hairdressing; photography by Ben Cook for TIGI; make-up by Amelia Pruen for TIGI; styling by Puschka and Jiv.) 56 (11), 60 (26), 63 (40), 65 (7 & 8), 67 (17), 72 (36), 73 (39), 81 (33), 92 (32, 33 & 34).

The Colour Room (Hair by Sean and James Tetlow; photography by Trevor Leighton and Jim Crone; make-up by Chase Aston, Cheryl Phelps-Gardiner, Ali Betts and Carol Wilson; styling by Peter Breen, Desiree Lederer and Charlotte Inghram.) 53 (left and centre), 54 (1), 55 (6 & 7), 56 (9, 10 & 12), 60 (24, 27 & 28), 64 (2), 66 (10, 11 & 12), 67 (14, 15 & 18), 75 (2 & 5), 78 (18 & 21), 84 (1), 85 (3), 88 (18), 89 (24).

The Hair Advice Centre
57 (15), 74 (1).

Webster Whiteman (Darren and Lisa at Webster Whiteman.) 57 (13 & 16), 60 (25 & 29), 61 (32), 63 (38), 65 (3), 69 (22), 77 (14), 82 (34 & 37), 85 (4), 90 (25 & 26), 91 (27 & 28).

Index

Figures in italics indicate captions.

Notes

Notes

Notes

Notes

Notes

Notes

Notes

Notes